THE DOLOURS OF
THE BLESSED VIRGIN MARY

The Dolours of the Blessed Virgin Mary

taken from
THE GLORIES OF MARY

TRANSLATED FROM THE ITALIAN OF

St Alphonsus Liguori

DOCTOR OF THE CHURCH AND FOUNDER OF THE
CONGREGATION OF THE MOST HOLY REDEEMER

CANA PRESS

This translation of *The Glories of Mary*, having been duly examined, is hereby approved of.

✠ JOHN,
Archbishop of New York
New York, Jan. 21st, 1852.

This book consists of an extract from
The Glories of Mary, originally published in 1852
by Edward Dunigan and Brother, New York.

Newly typeset and edited by Notre Dame Priory

Cana Press © 2026, all rights reserved.

No part of this book may be reproduced or transmitted, in any form or by any means, without permission.

For information, address:
PO Box 85,
Colebrook,
Tasmania, 7027,
Australia

canapress.com.au
notredamemonastery.org

ISBN
978-1-7644945-0-2

Protest Of The Author

In obedience to the decrees of Urban VIII, of holy memory, I protest that I do not intend to attribute any other than purely human authority to all the miracles, revelations, graces, and incidents contained in this book; neither to the titles holy or blessed applied to the servants of God not yet canonised; except in cases where these have been confirmed by the holy Roman Catholic Church, and by the holy Apostolic See, of whom I profess myself an obedient son; and therefore to their judgment I submit myself and whatever I have written in this book.

Contents

Protest Of The Author v
Petition Of The Author To Jesus And Mary ix
Prayer To The Blessed Virgin To Obtain A Good Death xi

On The Dolours of Mary 1

REFLECTIONS ON EACH OF THE SEVEN DOLOURS
OF MARY IN PARTICULAR

Of St Simeon's Prophecy 21
Of The Flight Of Jesus Into Egypt 29
Of The Loss Of Jesus In The Temple 35
Of The Meeting Of Mary With Jesus,
                When He Went To Death 43
Of The Death Of Jesus 51
The Piercing Of The Side Of Jesus,
                And His Descent From The Cross 59
The Burial Of The Body Of Jesus 67

Little Rosary Of The Seven Dolours Of Mary 73

Petition Of The Author To Jesus And Mary

My most loving Redeemer and Lord Jesus Christ, I thy poor servant, knowing how pleasing to thee are those who seek to glorify thy most holy mother, whom thou lovest so much, and dost so much desire to see loved and honoured by all men, I propose to publish this book of mine which treats of her glories. I know not to whom I could commend it but to thee, who hast so much at heart the glory of this mother. To thee, then, I present and dedicate it. Receive this little offering of my love for thee and thy beloved mother. Take it under thy protection, and pour into the hearts of those who read it the light of confidence in this immaculate Virgin, and the warmth of a burning love for her, in whom thou hast placed the hope and refuge of all the redeemed. And for the reward of this, my poor effort, give me, I pray thee, that love for Mary with which I have desired to inflame, by this my little work, the hearts of all those who read it.

To thee also I appeal, oh my sweetest Lady and mother Mary. Thou knowest that in thee, next to Jesus, I have placed all hope of my eternal salvation, since all the good I have received, my conversion, my vocation to leave the world, and whatever other graces have been given me by God, I acknowledge them all as coming through thee. Thou knowest that to see thee loved by all as thou dost deserve, and to offer thee some token of gratitude, I have always sought to proclaim thee everywhere, in public and in private, and to inspire all men with a sweet and salutary devotion to thee. I hope to continue to do so for the remainder of my life, even to my last breath. But I see by my advanced age and declining health that the end of my pilgrimage and my entrance into eternity are drawing near; therefore, I hope to give to the world, before my death, this little book of mine which may continue to proclaim thee for me, and also may excite others to publish thy glories and the great mercy which thou dost exercise towards thy devoted servants. I hope, my most beloved queen, that this my poor offering, although it falls so far short of thy merit, may be pleasing to thy grateful heart, since it is wholly a gift of love. Extend, then, that most kind hand of thine with which thou hast delivered me from the world and from hell, and accept it and protect it as belonging to thee. But I ask this reward for my little offering, that henceforth I may love thee more, and that all into whose hands this work shall fall, may be inflamed with thy love, so that immediately their desire may increase to love thee, and see others love thee also; and that they may engage with all ardour in proclaiming and promoting, as far as possible, thy praise, and confidence in thy most holy intercession. Thus I hope, thus may it be.

Prayer To The Blessed Virgin To Obtain A Good Death

Oh Mary, sweet refuge of miserable sinners, at the moment when my soul departs from this world, my sweetest mother, by the grief that thou didst endure when thou wast present at the death of thy Son upon the cross, then assist me with thy mercy. Keep far from me my infernal enemies, and come thyself to take my soul and present it to my eternal Judge. Do not abandon me, oh my queen. Thou, next to Jesus, must be my comfort in that dreadful moment. Entreat thy Son that in his goodness, he will grant me the favour to die clasping thy feet, and to breathe out my soul in his sacred wounds, saying, Jesus and Mary, I give you my heart and my soul.

On The Dolours of Mary

*Mary was queen of martyrs, because her martyrdom
was longer and greater than that of all the martyrs.*

Who can have a heart so hard that it will not melt on hearing of a most lamentable event which once happened in the world? There was a noble and holy mother who had but one only Son; and he was the most amiable that could be imagined, innocent, virtuous, beautiful, and most loving towards his mother; so much so, that he never had caused her the least displeasure, but always had showed her all respect, obedience, and affection. Hence the mother had placed on this Son all her earthly affections. Now what happened? It happened that this Son, through envy, was falsely accused by his enemies, and the judge, although he knew and confessed his innocence, yet, that he might not offend his enemies, condemned him to an infamous death, precisely as they had requested him to do. And this poor mother had to suffer the affliction of seeing that amiable and beloved Son so unjustly taken from her, in the flower of his age, by a barbarous death; for he was made to die in torment, drained of his blood before her own eyes, in a public place, upon an infamous gibbet. Devout souls, what do you say? Is this case and this unhappy mother worthy of compassion? Already you know of whom I speak. This Son so cruelly slain was our loving Redeemer, Jesus, and this mother was the blessed Virgin Mary, who, for love of us, was willing to see him offered up to the divine justice by the barbarity of men. This great pain, then, which Mary suffered for us—a pain which was more than a thousand deaths—merits our compassion and gratitude. And if we can return nothing else for so much love, at least let us, for a little time today, stop to consider the severity of the suffering by which Mary became queen of martyrs; for her great martyrdom exceeded in suffering that of all the martyrs,—being, in the first place, the longest martyrdom; and in the second place, the greatest martyrdom.

First Point.—As Jesus is called King of sorrows and King of martyrs, because he suffered in his life more than all the other martyrs, so is also Mary called, with reason, queen of the martyrs, having merited this title by suffering the greatest martyrdom that could be suffered, next to that of her Son. Hence she was justly named by Richard of St Laurence, the martyr of martyrs: '*Martyr martyrum*'.[1] And to her may be applied what Isaias said: He will crown thee with the crown of tribulation: '*Coronans coronabit te tribulatione.*'[2] For that suffering itself which exceeded the suffering of all the other martyrs

[1] EDITOR'S NOTE—This text contains numerous Latin texts and quotations both in the body of the text as well as the footnotes. Where a Latin text is given in the body it is generally preceded by an English translation e.g. '*Martyr martyrum*' means 'the martyr of martyrs'. Similarly, whenever there is a Latin quotation in a footnote, it is giving the original Latin of whichever quote is being referenced.

[2] Is 22:18.

united, was the crown by which she was shown to be the queen of martyrs. That Mary was a true martyr cannot be doubted, as is proved by Denis the Carthusian, Pelbart, Catharinus, and others; for it is an established opinion that suffering sufficient to cause death, constitutes martyrdom, although death may not then take place. St John the Evangelist is revered as a martyr, although he did not die in the cauldron of boiling oil, but came out more sound than he went in: *'Vegetior exiverit quam intraverit.'*[1] It is sufficient to procure the glory of martyrdom, says St Thomas, that anyone should be obedient even to offer himself to death.[2] Mary was a martyr, says St Bernard, not by the sword of the executioner, but by the bitter sorrow of her heart.[3] If her body was not wounded by the hand of the executioner, yet her blessed heart was pierced by grief at the passion of her Son; a grief sufficient to cause her not only one, but a thousand deaths. And from this we shall see that Mary was not only a true martyr, but that her martyrdom surpassed that of all the other martyrs, for it was a longer martyrdom, and, if I may thus express it, all her life was a long death.

The passion of Jesus commenced with his birth, as St Bernard says;[4] and Mary also, in all things like unto her Son, suffered her martyrdom through her whole life. The name of Mary, among its other significations, as the blessed Albertus Magnus affirms, signifies a *bitter sea*: '*Mare amarum*'. Wherefore to her is applied the passage of Jeremias: Great as the sea is thy destruction: *'Magna est enim velut mare contritio tua.'*[5] For as the sea is all salt and bitter, thus the life of Mary was always full of bitterness at the sight of the passion of the Redeemer,

[1] Brev. Rom. 6, Maj.
[2] Martyrium amplectitur id quod in obedientia summum esse potest, ut scilicet aliquis sit obediens usque ad mortem. 2a 2æ, q. 134, a. 3, ad 3.
[3] Non ferro carnificis, sed acerbo dolore cordis. Ap. Baldi. tom. 1, p. 146.
[4] A nativitatis exordio, passio crucis simul exorta. Serm. 2, de Pass.
[5] Thr. 2:13.

which was ever present to her. It cannot be doubted that being more enlightened by the Holy Spirit than all the prophets, she better comprehended than they the predictions concerning the Messias, which they recorded in their holy Scriptures. Precisely this the angel revealed to St Bridget.[1] Whence, as the same angel declared, the Virgin knowing how much the incarnate Word was to suffer for the salvation of men, even before she became his mother, and compassionating this innocent Saviour, who was to be so cruelly put to death for crimes not his own, she commenced, from that time, her great martyrdom.[2]

Her grief afterwards increased immeasurably when she was made mother of this Saviour. So that at the painful thought of all the sufferings which her poor Son was to endure, she indeed experienced, says Rupert the Abbot, a long martyrdom—a martyrdom continued through her whole life.[3] And exactly this was signified by the vision which St Bridget had at Rome, in the church of St Mary Major, where the blessed Virgin appeared to her with St Simeon, and an angel, having a sword which was very long and red with blood; by which was prefigured the long and bitter grief that pierced the heart of Mary during her whole life.[4] Whence the above-named Rupert puts into the mouth of Mary the following words: 'Oh redeemed souls and my beloved children, do not pity me only for that hour in which I saw my dear Jesus dying in my presence, for the sword of sorrow, predicted to me by Simeon, pierced my soul during my whole life; when I was giving suck to my Son, when I was

---

[1] Proculdubio est credendum, quod ipsa ex inspiratione Spiritus Sancti perfectius intellexit quicquid Prophetarum eloquia figurabant. Serm. Ang. c. 17.
[2] Ex Scripturis Deum incarnari intelligens, et quod tam diversis pœnis deberet cruciari, tribulationem non modicam sustinuit. Serm. Ang. c. 16.
[3] Tu longum præscia futuræ passionis filii tui, pertulisti martyrium. In Cant. 4.
[4] Rev. l. 7, c. 2.

warming him in my arms, I already saw the bitter death that awaited him; consider then what long and cruel sorrows I must have endured.'[1]

Wherefore Mary might truly say in the words of David: 'My life is wasted with grief and my years in sighs.'[2] My sorrow is continually before me: *'Dolor meus in conspectu meo semper.'*[3] My life was wholly passed in grief and tears; for my grief, which was compassion for my beloved Son, never departed from before my eyes, seeing, as I did, continually the sufferings and death that he was one day to endure. The divine mother herself revealed to St Bridget, that even after the death and ascension of her Son into heaven, the memory of his passion, whether she ate or worked, was deeply impressed and ever recent in her tender heart.[4] Tauler therefore says, that Mary passed her whole life in perpetual sorrow; for her heart was always occupied with thoughts of sadness and of suffering.[5]

So that time, which usually mitigates the sorrows of the afflicted, did not relieve Mary; nay, time itself increased her sorrow, for as Jesus increased in years, on the one hand, he continually showed himself more lovely and amiable; and on the other, the time of his death was ever drawing nearer, and grief at having to lose him on this earth, continually increased in the heart of Mary. As the rose grows up among thorns, said the angel to St Bridget, so the mother of God advanced in years

---

[1] Nolite solam attendere horam illam qua dilectum meum vidi mori; nam Simeonis gladius, antequam pertransiret, longum per me transitum fecit. Cum igitur eum lactarem, foverem et prospicerem ejus mortem, quam prolixam me putatis pertulisse passionem? Loc. cit.

[2] Defecit in dolore vita mea, et anni mei in gemitibus. Ps. 30: 11.

[3] Ps. 37:18.

[4] Tempore quo post ascensionem filii mei vixi, passio sua in corde meo fixa erat, ut sive comedebam, sive laborabam, quasi recens erat in memoria mea. Rev. l. 6, c. 65.

[5] Beatissima Virgo pro tota vita fecit professionem doloris. Vit. Christ. c. 28.

in the midst of sufferings; and as the thorns increase with the growth of the rose, thus this rose selected by the Lord, Mary, as she increased in age, was so much the more pierced by the thorns of her dolours.[1] Having considered the length of this suffering, let us now pass on to the second point, namely, the consideration of its greatness.

Second Point.—Ah, Mary was not only queen of the martyrs, because her martyrdom was longer than that of all others, but also because it was the greatest of all. But who can measure its greatness? Jeremias appears to be unable to find anyone with whom he may compare this mother of sorrows, when considering her great suffering at the death of her Son. 'To what shall I compare thee, or to what shall I liken thee, oh daughter of Jerusalem; for great as the sea is thy destruction; who shall heal thee?'[2] Wherefore Cardinal Hugo, commenting on these words, says: Oh blessed Virgin, as the bitterness of the sea exceeds all other bitterness, so thy grief surpasses all other griefs.[3] Hence St Anselm affirms, that if God, by a special miracle, had not preserved the life of Mary, her grief would have been sufficient to cause her death at each moment of her life.[4] And St Bernardine of Sienna even says, that the grief of Mary was so great, that if it were divided among all men, it would be enough to cause their immediate death.[5]

---

[1] Sicut rosa crescere solet inter spinas ita B. Virgo in hoc mundo crevit inter tribulationes; et sicut, crescente rosa, crescunt spinæ; sic hæc electissima rosa Maria, quanto crescebat ætate, tanto tribulationum spinis pungebatur. Serm. Ang. c. 16.

[2] Cui comparabo te? vel cui assimilabo te, filia Jerusalem? Magna est enim velut mare contritio tua. Quis medebitur tui? Lam. 2:1.

[3] Quemadmodum mare est in amaritudine excellens, ita tuæ contritioni nulla calamitas æquari potest.

[4] Utique, Domina, non crediderim te potuisse stimulos tanti cruciatus, quin vitam amitteres, sustinere; nisi ipse spiritus tui filii te confortaret. De Ec. Virg. c. 3.

[5] Tantus fuit dolor Virginis, quod si inter omnes creaturas, quæ dolorem

But let us consider the reasons why the martyrdom of Mary was greater than that of all the martyrs. In the first place, it must be remembered that the martyrs suffered their martyrdom in the body, by means of fire or steel; Mary suffered martyrdom in her soul, as St Simeon had before prophesied: And thy own soul a sword shall pierce, '*Et tuam ipsius animam pertransibit gladius,*'[1] as if the holy old man had said to her: 'Oh holy Virgin, the bodies of the other martyrs will be torn with iron, but thou wilt be pierced and martyred in thy soul, by the passion of thy own Son.' Now, as the soul is more noble than the body, so much greater was the suffering of Mary than that of all the martyrs; as Jesus Christ himself said to St Catherine of Sienna: There is no comparison between the sufferings of the soul and the body: '*Inter dolorem animæ et corporis nulla est comparatio.*' Whence the holy abbot Arnold Carnotensis says, that whoever had been present on Calvary at the great sacrifice of the immaculate Lamb, when he was dying on the cross, would have there beheld two great altars, one in the body of Jesus, the other in the heart of Mary; for there, at the same time that the Son sacrificed his body in death, Mary sacrificed her soul in compassion.[2]

Moreover, while the other martyrs, as St Antoninus says,[3] suffered by sacrificing their own lives, the blessed Virgin suffered by sacrificing the life of her Son, whom she loved far more than her own life; so that she not only suffered in spirit all that her Son suffered in body, but, moreover, the sight of the sufferings of her Son brought more grief to her heart than if she had endured them all in her own person. There can be no doubt that Mary suffered in her heart all the tortures by which she saw her

---

pati possunt, divideretur, omnes subito interirent. To. 1, Serm. 67.

[1] Lk. 2:35.
[2] Nimirum in tabernaculo illo duo videres altaria, aliud in pectore matris, aliud in corpore Christi; Christus carnem, Maria immolabat animam. Tr. de sep. verb. Do. in Cru.
[3] P. 1, tit. 15, c. 24.

beloved Jesus tormented. Everyone knows that the sufferings of children are also the sufferings of their mothers, when they are the witnesses of them. St Augustine, considering the anguish that the mother of the Macchabees experienced in witnessing the tortures which her sons endured, says: 'She suffered in them all, because she loved them all; and endured with her eyes what they all endured in the flesh.'[1] Thus also was it with Mary; all those torments, scourgings, thorns, nails, and the cross, which tortured the innocent flesh of Jesus, entered at the same time into the heart of Mary to complete her martyrdom. He in the flesh, she in the heart suffered, writes St Amadeus: '*Ille carne, illa corde passa est.*'[2] So that, as St Lawrence Justinian says, the heart of Mary became as it were a mirror of the agonies of her Son, in which were seen the spitting, the scourging, the wounds, and all that Jesus suffered.[3] And St Bonaventure remarks that these wounds which were scattered all over the body of Jesus, were all united in the one heart of Mary.[4]

The Virgin, then, through compassion for her Son, was scourged, crowned with thorns, insulted, and nailed to the cross. Whence the same saint considering Mary on Mt Calvary, where she was present with her dying Son, asks of her: 'Oh Lady, tell me where you then stood? Perhaps only at the foot of the cross! Might I not rather say thou wast on the cross itself crucified with thy Son?'[5] And Richard, remarking on the words of the Redeemer, which he spoke by the mouth of Isaias: 'I have

---

[1] Illa videndo in omnibus passa est; quia amabat omnes, ferebat in oculis quod in carne omnes. Serm. 109, de Divers. c. 6.
[2] Hom. 5.
[3] Passionis Christi speculum effectum erat cor Virginis, in illo agnoscebantur sputa, convicia, verbera, vulnera. De Agon. Chri. c. 11.
[4] Singula vulnera per ejus corpus dispersa, in uno corde sunt unita. De Planctu. Virg. in Stim. Am.
[5] O Domina mea ubi stabas? Nunquid tantum juxta crucem? Imo in cruce cum filio crucifixa eras. Loc. cit.

trodden the wine-press alone, and of the Gentiles there is not a man with me,'¹ adds: 'Oh Lord, thou dost rightly say that in the work of human redemption thou didst suffer alone, and there was no man that could pity thee sufficiently; but there was a woman with thee, thy own mother, who suffered in her heart whatever thou didst suffer in thy body.'²

But all this is saying only too little of the sorrows of Mary; for, as I have before said, she suffered more in seeing her beloved Jesus suffer, than if in her own person she had endured all the tortures and the death of her Son. Erasmus has written, speaking of parents, generally, that they feel the sufferings of their children more than their own.³ But this is not always true. It was no doubt true of Mary, for she certainly loved her Son and his life far more than herself, and a thousand lives of her own. Therefore St Amadeus well declares, that the afflicted mother, at the sorrowful sight of the agony of her beloved Jesus, suffered much more than if she herself had endured his whole passion.⁴ The reason is plain, since, as St Bernard says: The soul is more where it loves, than where it lives: *'Anima magis est ubi amat, quam ubi animat.'* And the Saviour himself had before said, that our heart is where our treasure is.⁵ If Mary, then, through love, lived more in her Son than in herself, a much greater grief did she suffer at the death of her Son, than if the most cruel death in the world had been inflicted on her.

And here is to be considered the other circumstance that rendered the martyrdom of Mary far greater than the sufferings

---

[1] Torcular calcavi solus, et de gentibus non est vir mecum. Is. 63:3.
[2] Verum est, Domine, quod non est vir tecum, sed mulier una est tecum, quæ omnia vulnera quæ tu suscepisti in corpore, suscepit in corde.
[3] Parentes atrocius torquentur in liberis, quam in scipsis. Libell. de Machab.
[4] Maria torquebatur magis, quam si torqueretur ex se; quoniam supra se incomparabiliter diligebat id unde dolebat. Cit. Hom. 5.
[5] Ubi thesaurus vester est, ibi et cor vestrum erit. Lk. 12:34.

of all the martyrs, for in the passion of Jesus she suffered much, and she suffered without alleviation. The martyrs suffered under the torments which their tyrants inflicted upon them, but love to Jesus rendered their pains sweet and delightful. A St Vincent suffered in his martyrdom; he was tortured on the rack, torn with hooks, burned with red-hot iron plates; but St Augustine says: One seemed to suffer, and another to speak: '*Alius videbatur pati, alius loqui.*' The saint addressed the tyrant with such power, and with such contempt of his torments, that it seemed as if one Vincent suffered and another Vincent spoke, so greatly did his God, with the sweetness of his love, comfort him in the midst of his sufferings. A St Boniface suffered; his body was torn with irons, sharp-pointed reeds were thrust between his nails and flesh, melted lead was poured into his mouth, and at the same time he could not often enough repeat: I give thanks to thee, oh Jesus Christ: '*Gratias tibi ago, Domine Jesu Christe.*' A St Mark and a St Marcellinus suffered; they were bound to a stake, their feet pierced by nails, and the tyrant appealed to them, saying: 'Miserable beings, look at your condition, and save yourselves from these torments.' And they answered: 'What torments, what pains do you speak of? We have never feasted with more joy than now, when we are suffering with pleasure for the love of Jesus Christ.'[1] A St Lawrence suffered, but while he was burning on the gridiron, the interior flame of love, as St Leo says, was more powerful to cheer his soul, than the flames without were to torture his body.[2] Hence love made him so strong, that he even braved the tyrant by saying to him: Tyrant, if you wish to feed on my flesh, a part is sufficiently cooked, turn and eat: '*Assatum est jam, versa et manduca.*' But in such torture and lingering death, how could the saint thus exult? Ah,

---

[1] Nunquam tam jucunde epulati sumus, quam cum hæc libenter Jesu Christi amore perferimus.

[2] Segnior fuit ignis qui foris ussit, quam qui intus accendit. In Nat. S. Laur.

St Augustine answers, because, intoxicated with the wine of divine love, he felt neither torments nor death.[1]

For the holy martyrs, the more they loved Jesus, the less they felt torments and death, and the sight alone of the sufferings of a crucified God was sufficient to console them. But was not our afflicted mother, also, thus consoled by love for her Son, and the sight of his sufferings? No, for this very Son who suffered, was the whole cause of her grief; and the love she bore him was her only, and too cruel executioner; for the whole martyrdom of Mary consisted in seeing and pitying her innocent and beloved Son, who suffered so much. Therefore, the more she loved him, the more bitter and inconsolable was her sorrow. 'Great as the sea is thy destruction, who shall heal thee?'[2] Ah, queen of heaven, love hath alleviated the sufferings of other martyrs, and has healed their wounds; but who has ever soothed thy great sorrow? Who has ever healed the cruel wounds of thy heart? Who will heal thee? '*Quis medebitur tui?*' If that same Son, who could give thee consolation, was by his sufferings the sole cause of thy sorrows, and the love that thou didst bear him, caused all thy martyrdom? Therefore, whilst the other martyrs, as Diez remarks, are all represented with the instrument of their passion—St Paul with the sword, St Andrew with the cross, St Lawrence with the gridiron—Mary is represented with her dead Son in her arms, because Jesus himself alone was the instrument of her martyrdom, by reason of the love which she bore him. In a few words St Bernard confirms all I have said: 'With the other martyrs their great love soothed the anguish of their martyrdom; but the more the blessed Virgin loved, so much the more she suffered, and so much more cruel was her martyrdom.'[3]

---

[1] In illa longa morte, in illis tormentis illo calice ebrius tormenta non sentit. Tract. 27.

[2] Magna est velut mare contritio tua; quis medebitur tui?

[3] In aliis martyribus magnitudo amoris dolorem lenivit passionis; sed bea-

It is certain that the greater is our love for a thing, the greater pain we feel in losing it. The loss of a brother certainly afflicts us more than the loss of a beast of burden; and the death of a son, more than that of a friend. Now Cornelius à Lapide says, that to comprehend how great was the grief of Mary at the death of her Son, we should comprehend how great was the love she bore him.[1] But who can measure that love? The blessed Amadeus says that in the heart of Mary two kinds of love to her Jesus were united: the supernatural love with which she loved him as her God, and the natural love with which she loved him as her son;[2] so that, of these two loves, one only was formed, but a love so immense that William of Paris even said, that the blessed Virgin loved Jesus to such a degree that a pure creature could not love him more.[3] And Richard of St Laurence says as there was no love like her love, so there was no grief like her grief.[4] If, therefore, the love of Mary for her Son was immense, immense, also, must have been her grief in losing him by death. Where love is greatest, says blessed Albertus Magnus, there grief is greatest: '*Ubi summus amor, ibi summus dolor.*'

Let us imagine, then, that the divine mother, standing near her Son dying upon the cross, and justly applying to herself the words of Jeremias, says to us: 'Oh, all ye that pass by the way attend, and see if there be any sorrow like to my sorrow.'[5] Oh ye that are passing your lives upon this earth, and have no

---

ta Virgo quanto plus amavit, tanto plus doluit, tantoque ipsius martyrium gravius fuit. Ap. Crois. Vit. Mar. s. 23.

[1] Ut scias quantus fuerit dolor B. Virginis, cogita quantus fuerit amor.
[2] Duæ dilectiones in unam convenerant et ex duobus amoribus factus est amor unus, cum Virgo mater filio divinitatis amorem impenderet, et in Deo amorem nato exhiberet. Hom. 5, de Laud. V.
[3] Quantum capere potuit puri hominis modus.
[4] Unde sicut non fuit amor sicut amor ejus, ita non fuit dolor sicut dolor ejus.
[5] O vos omnes qui transitas per viam attendite, et videte, si est dolor sicut dolor meus. Lam. 1:12.

pity for me, stop a while to look upon me, now that I behold this beloved Son dying before my eyes; and then see if among all who are afflicted and tormented, there be sorrow like to my sorrow. No, answers St Bonaventure, there can be found no sorrow, oh afflicted mother, more bitter than thine, for no son can be found more dear than thine.[1] Ah, there has never been in the world, says St Lawrence Justinian, a son more worthy of love than Jesus, nor a mother who loved her son more than Mary; if, then, there has never been in the world a love like the love of Mary, how can there be a grief like the grief of Mary?[2]

Therefore St Ildephonsus did not hesitate to affirm, that it was little to say that the sufferings of the Virgin exceeded all the torments of the martyrs, even were they united together.[3] And St Anselm adds, that the most cruel tortures inflicted upon the holy martyrs were light or nothing, in comparison with the martyrdom of Mary.[4] St Basil likewise writes, that as the sun surpasses in splendour all the other planets, so Mary in her sufferings exceeded the sufferings of all the other martyrs.[5] A certain learned author[6] concludes with an admirable sentiment, saying, that so great was the sorrow which this tender mother suffered in the passion of Jesus, that she alone could worthily compassionate the death of a God made man.

But St Bonaventure, addressing the blessed Virgin, says: Oh Lady, why hast thou wished to go and sacrifice thyself also on

[1] Nullus dolor amarior, quia nulla proles charior. De Compas. Virg. c. 2.
[2] Non fuit talis filius, non fuit talis mater; non fuit tanta charitas, non fuit dolor tantus. Ideo quanto dilexit tenerius, tanta vulnerata est profundius. Lib. 3, de Laud. Virg.
[3] Parum est Mariam in passione filii tam acerbos pertulisse dolores, ut omnium martyrum collective tormenta superaret. Ap. Sinisc. Mart. de Mar. Cons. 36.
[4] Quicquid crudelitatis inflictum est corporibus martyrum, leve fuit, aut potius nihil comparatione tuæ passionis. De Exc. Virg. c. 5.
[5] Virgo universos martyres tantum excedit, quantum sol reliqua astra.
[6] P. Pinam.

Calvary? Was not a crucified God sufficient to redeem us, that thou his mother wouldst be crucified also?[1] Indeed, the death of Jesus was more than enough to save the world, and also an infinity of worlds; but this good mother wished, for the love she bore us, likewise to aid the cause of our salvation with the merits of the sorrows which she offered for us on Calvary. And, therefore, says the blessed Albertus Magnus, as we are indebted to Jesus for what he suffered for love of us, we are also indebted to Mary for the martyrdom which she, in the death of her Son, voluntarily suffered for our salvation.[2] I have added voluntarily, since, as the angel revealed to St Bridget, this our so merciful and kind mother was willing to suffer any pain, rather than to see souls unredeemed or left in their former perdition.[3] It may be said that this was the only consolation of Mary in the midst of her great sorrow at the passion of her Son, to see the lost world redeemed by his death, and men, who were his enemies, reconciled with God. Grieving, she rejoiced, says Simon da Cassia, because the sacrifice was offered for the redemption of all, by which wrath was appeased.[4]

Such love as that of Mary merits our gratitude, and let us show our gratitude by meditating upon and compassionating her sorrows. But of this she complained to St Bridget, that very few pitied her, and most lived forgetful of her sorrows. 'I look around upon all who are in the world, if perchance there may be any to pity me, and meditate upon my sorrows, and truly I find very few. Therefore, my daughter, though I am forgotten

[1] O Domina, cur ivisti immolari pro nobis? Non sufficiebat filii passio, nisi crucifigeretur et mater? Ap. Pac. Exc. 10, in Sal. Ang.
[2] Sicut totus mundus obligatur Deo propter passionem, sic obligatur Dominæ propter compassionem. Sup. Miss. cap. 20.
[3] Sic pia et misericors est, et fuit, quod maluit omnes tribulationes sufferre, quam quod animæ non redimerentur. Rev. l. 3, c. 30.
[4] Lætabatur dolens quod offerebatur sacrificium in redemptionem omnium quo placabatur iratus. De Gest. D. l. 2. c. 27.

by many, at least do not thou forget me; behold my anguish, and imitate, as far as thou canst, my grief.'[1] In order to understand how much the Virgin is pleased by our remembrance of her dolours, it is sufficient to relate that, in the year 1239, she appeared to seven of her servants, who then became the founders of the order of the Servants of Mary, with a black garment in her hand, and told them that if they wished to please her, they should often meditate upon her dolours; and therefore she wished, in memory of them, that they would hereafter wear that garment of mourning.[2] And Jesus Christ himself revealed to the blessed Veronica Binasco, that he takes more pleasure, as it were, in seeing his mother compassionated than himself; for thus he addressed her: 'My daughter, the tears shed for my passion are dear to me; but loving with so great love my mother Mary, the meditation of the dolours which she suffered at my death is more dear to me.'[3]

Wherefore the graces are very great which Jesus promises to those who are devoted to the dolours of Mary. Pelbart relates,[4] that it was revealed to St Elizabeth, that St John the Evangelist, after the blessed Virgin was assumed into heaven, desired to see her again. This favour was granted him; his dear mother appeared to him, and Jesus Christ with her; and he then heard Mary asking of her Son some peculiar grace for those who were devoted to her dolours; and Jesus promised her for them the four following special graces: First, that those who invoke the divine mother by her sorrows, before death will merit to obtain true repentance of all their sins. Second, that he will protect

[1] Respicio ad omnes qui in mundo sunt, si forte sint aliqui qui compatiantur mihi, et recogitent dolorem meum; et valde paucos invenio. Ideo filia mea, licet a multis oblita sim, tu tamen non obliviscaris mei, vide dolorem meum, et imitare quantum potes, et dole. Rev. l. 2, c. 24.
[2] Gian. Cent. Serv. l. 1, c. 14.
[3] Ap. Bolland. 13, Jan.
[4] Stellar. l. 3, p. 3, a. 3.

such in their tribulations, especially at the hour of death. Third, that he will impress upon them the memory of his passion, and that they shall have their reward for it in heaven. Fourth, that he will commit such devout servants to the hands of Mary, that she may dispose of them according to her pleasure, and obtain for them all the graces she desires. In proof of this, let us see in the following example how devotion to the dolours of Mary may aid our eternal salvation.

EXAMPLE

We read in the revelations of St Bridget,[1] that there was once a lord as noble by birth as he was low and sinful in his habits. He had given himself by an express compact as a slave to the devil, and had served him for sixty successive years, leading such a life as may easily be imagined, and never approaching the sacraments. Now, this prince was about to die, and Jesus Christ, in his compassion, commanded St Bridget to tell his confessor to visit him, and exhort him to make his confession. The confessor went, and the sick man told him that he had no need of a confessor, for that he had often made his confession. The confessor visited him a second time, and that poor slave of hell persevered in his obstinate determination not to make his confession. Jesus again directed the saint to tell the confessor to go to him again. He obeyed, and this third time related to him the revelation made to the saint, and that he had returned so many times because the Lord, who desired to show him mercy, had directed him to do so. On hearing this, the dying man was moved, and began to weep. But how, he exclaimed, can I be pardoned, when for sixty years I have served the devil, made myself his slave, and have laden my soul with innumerable sins? 'Son,' answered the father, encouraging him, 'do not doubt: if you repent of them, in the name of God I promise you pardon.'

[1] L. 6, c. 97.

Then beginning to gain confidence, he said to the confessor: 'Father, I believed myself lost, and despaired of salvation; but now I feel a sorrow for my sins, which encourages me to trust; and as God has not yet abandoned me, I wish to make my confession.' And in fact on that day he made his confession four times, with great sorrow; the next day he received communion, and on the sixth he died, contrite and entirely resigned. After his death, Jesus Christ further revealed to St Bridget, that this sinner was saved, and was in purgatory, and that he had been saved by the intercession of the Virgin, his mother; for the deceased, although he had led so sinful a life, yet had always preserved devotion to her dolours, whenever he remembered them he pitied her.

PRAYER

Oh my afflicted mother! Queen of martyrs and of sorrows, thou hast shed so many tears for thy Son, who died for my salvation, and yet what will thy tears avail me, if I am lost? By the merits, then, of thy dolours, obtain for me a true sorrow for my sins, and a true amendment of life, with a perpetual and tender compassion for the passion of Jesus and thy own sufferings. And if Jesus and thou, being so innocent, have suffered so much for me, obtain for me that I, who am deserving of hell, may also suffer something for love of you. Oh Lady, I will say to thee with St Bonaventure, if I have offended thee, wound my heart in punishment; if I have served thee, now I beg to be wounded as a reward. It is a shameful thing to see our Lord Jesus wounded, and thee wounded with him, and I uninjured.[1] Finally, oh my mother, by the grief thou didst experience on seeing thy Son before thy eyes bow his head and expire upon

---

[1] O Domina, si te offendi pro justitia cor meum vulnera; si tibi servivi, nunc pro mercede, peto, vulnera. Opprobriosum est videre Dominum Jesum vulneratum, te convulneratum, et me illæsum.

the cross, I entreat of thee to obtain for me a good death. Ah, do not cease, oh advocate of sinners, to assist my afflicted and struggling soul in that great passage that it has to make into eternity. And, because at that time it may easily be the case that I shall have lost the use of speech with which to invoke thy name, and that of Jesus, who are all my hope, therefore I now invoke thy Son and thee to succour me at that last moment, and I say: Jesus and Mary, to you I commend my soul. Amen.

Reflections On Each Of The Seven Dolours Of Mary In Particular

On The First Dolour
Of St Simeon's Prophecy

In this valley of tears, every man is born to weep, and everyone must suffer those afflictions that daily befall him. But how much more miserable would life be, if everyone knew also the future evils which are to afflict him! Too unhappy would he be, says Seneca, whose fate was such.[1] The Lord exercises this compassion towards us, namely, that he does not make known to us the crosses that await us; that if we are to suffer them, at least we may suffer them only once. But he did not exercise this compassion with Mary, who, because God wished her to be queen of dolours, and in all things like his Son, had to see always before her eyes, and to suffer continually all the sorrows that awaited her; and those were the sufferings of the passion and death of her beloved Jesus. For St Simeon in the temple, after having received the divine child in his arms,

[1] Calamitosus esset animus futuri præscius et ante miserias miser. Ep. 98.

predicted to her that this child was to be the mark for all the opposition and persecution of men: 'Set for a sign which shall be contradicted;' and that therefore the sword of sorrow should pierce her soul: 'And thy own soul a sword shall pierce.'[1]

The holy Virgin herself said to St Matilda, that at this announcement of St Simeon all her joy was changed into sorrow.[2] For, as it was revealed to St Teresa, the blessed mother, although she knew before this that the life of her Son would be sacrificed for the salvation of the world, yet she then learned more particularly and distinctly the sufferings and cruel death that awaited her poor Son. She knew that he would be contradicted in all things. Contradicted in doctrine; for instead of being believed, he would be esteemed a blasphemer for teaching that he was the Son of God, as the impious Caiaphas declared him to be, saying: 'He hath blasphemed, he is guilty of death.'[3] Contradicted in his reputation, for he was noble, of royal lineage, and was despised as a peasant: 'Is not this the carpenter's son?'[4] 'Is not this the carpenter, the son of Mary?'[5] He was wisdom itself, and was treated as an ignorant man: 'How doth this man know letters, having never learned?'[6] As a false prophet: 'And they blindfolded him and smote his face ... saying: Prophesy who is this that struck thee.'[7] He was treated as a madman: 'He is mad, why hear you him?'[8] As a wine-bibber, a glutton, and a friend of sinners: 'Behold a man that is a glutton, and a drinker

---

[1] Positus est hic in signum cui contradicetur. Et tuam ipsius animam doloris gladius pertransibit. Lk. 2:35.
[2] Omnis lætitia mea ad illa verba in mœrore conversa est.
[3] Blasphemavit, reus est mortis. Matt. 26:65, 66.
[4] Non hic fabri filius? Matt. 13:55.
[5] Nonne hic est faber, filius Mariæ? Matt. 6:3.
[6] Quomodo hic literas scit, cum non didicerit. Jn. 7:15.
[7] Et velaverunt eum, et percutiebant faciem ejus ... dicentes; Prophetiza, quis est qui te percussit. Lk. 22:64.
[8] Insanit, quid eum auditis? Jn. 10:20.

of wine, a friend of publicans and sinners.'[1] As a sorcerer: 'By the prince of devils he casteth out devils.'[2] As a heretic and possessed person: 'Do we not say well of thee, that thou art a Samaritan, and hast a devil?'[3] In a word, Jesus was considered as so bad and notorious a man, that no trial was necessary to condemn him, as the Jews said to Pilate: 'If he were not a malefactor, we would not have delivered him up to thee.'[4] He was contradicted in his soul, for even his eternal Father, in order to give place to the divine justice, contradicted him by not wishing to hear him when he prayed to him, saying: 'Father, if it be possible, let this chalice pass from me;'[5] and abandoned him to fear, weariness, and sadness, so that our afflicted Lord said: 'My soul is sorrowful even unto death.'[6] His interior suffering even caused him to sweat blood. Contradicted and persecuted, in a word, in his body and his life, for he was tortured in all his sacred members: in his hands, in his feet, in his face, in his head, in his whole body, till, drained to the last drop of his blood, he died an ignominious death on the cross.

When David, in the midst of all his pleasures and royal grandeur, heard from Nathan the prophet that his son should die—'The child that is born to thee shall surely die'[7]—he could find no peace, but wept, fasted, and slept upon the ground. Mary received with the greatest calmness the announcement that her Son should die, and peacefully continued to submit to it; but what grief she must have continually suffered, seeing this

---

[1] Ecce homo devorator, et bibens vinum, amicus publicanorum et peccatorum. Lk. 7:34.
[2] In principe dæmoniorum ejicit dæmonia. Matt. 9:34.
[3] Nonne bene dicimus nos, quia Samaritanus es tu, et dæmonium habes? Jn. 8:48.
[4] Si non esset hic malefactor, non tibi tradidissemus eum. Jn. 18:30.
[5] Pater mi, si possibile est, transeat a me calix iste. Matt.26:39.
[6] Tristis es anima mea usque ad mortem. Matt. 26:38.
[7] Filius qui natus est tibi, morte morietur. 2 Kings 12:14.

amiable Son always near her, hearing from him words of eternal life, and beholding his holy demeanour. Abraham suffered great affliction during the three days he passed with his beloved Isaac, after he knew that he was to lose him. Oh God! Not for three days, but for thirty-three years, Mary had to endure a like sorrow. Like, do I say? A sorrow as much greater as the Son of Mary was more lovely than the son of Abraham. The blessed Virgin herself revealed to St Bridget,[1] that while she lived on the earth there was not an hour when this grief did not pierce her soul: As often, she continued, as I looked upon my Son, as often as I wrapped him in his swaddling clothes, as often as I saw his hands and his feet, so often was my soul overwhelmed as it were with a fresh sorrow, because I considered how he would be crucified.[2] Rupert the Abbot, contemplating Mary, while she was suckling her Son, imagines her addressing him in these words: 'A bundle of myrrh is my beloved to me, he shall abide between my breasts.'[3] Ah, my Son, I clasp thee in my arms, because thou art so dear to me; but the dearer thou art to me, the more thou dost become to me a bundle of myrrh and of sorrow, when I think of thy sufferings. Mary, says St Bernardine of Sienna,[4] considered that the strength of the saints was to pass through death; the beauty of paradise to be deformed; the Lord of the universe to be bound as a criminal; the Creator of all things to be livid with stripes; the Judge of all to be condemned; the glory of heaven despised; the King of kings to be crowned with thorns, and treated as a mock king.

---

[1] Lib. 6, Rev. c. 9.
[2] Quoties aspiciebam filium meum, quoties involvebam eum pannis, quoties videbam ejus manus et pedes; toties animus meus quasi novo dolore absorptus est; quia cogitabam, quomodo crucifigeretur. Lib. 6, c. 57.
[3] Fasciculus mirrhæ dilectus meus mihi, inter ubera mea commorabitur. Cant. 1:12.
[4] Tom. 3, Serm. 2, a. 3, c. 1.

Father Engelgrave writes that it was revealed to the same St Bridget that the afflicted mother, knowing all that her Son would have to suffer, when suckling him, thought of the gall and vinegar; when she swathed him, of the cords with which he was to be bound; when she bore him in her arms, she thought of him being nailed to the cross; and when he slept, she thought of his death.[1] As often as she put on him his clothes, she reflected that they would one day be torn from him, that he might be crucified; and when she beheld his sacred hands and feet, and thought of the nails that were to pierce them, as Mary said to St Bridget: 'My eyes filled with tears, and my heart was tortured with grief.'[2]

The evangelist says that as Jesus Christ advanced in years, so also he advanced in wisdom and in grace with God and men.[3] That is, he advanced in wisdom and in grace before men, or in their estimation; and before God, according to St Thomas,[4] inasmuch as all his works would continually have availed to increase his merit, if from the beginning grace in its complete fullness had not been conferred on him by virtue of the hypostatic union. But if Jesus advanced in the esteem and love of others, how much more did he advance in Mary's love! But, oh God, as love increased in her, the more increased in her the grief of having to lose him by a death so cruel. And the nearer the time of the passion of her Son approached, with so much greater pain did that sword of sorrow, predicted by St

---

[1] Eum lactans cogitabat de felle et aceto; quando fasciis involvebat, funes cogitabat quibus ligandus erat; quando gestabat, cogitabat in cruce confixum; quando dormiebat, cogitabat mortuum. Tom. 1, Ev. Lu. Dom. infr. Oct. Nat. s. 1.

[2] Oculi mei replebantur lacrymis, et cor meum torquebatur dolore. Lib. 6, c. 57, et l. 7, c. 7.

[3] Et Jesus proficiebat sapientia et ætate, et gratia apud Deum, et homines. Lk. 2:23.

[4] ST 3a, q. 7, art. 12.

Simeon, pierce the heart of the mother; precisely this the angel revealed to St Bridget, saying: 'That sword of sorrow was every hour drawing nearer to the Virgin as the time for the passion of her Son drew nearer.'[1]

If, then, Jesus our King and his most holy mother did not refuse, for love of us, to suffer during their whole life such cruel pains, there is no reason that we should complain if we suffer a little. Jesus crucified once appeared to sister Magdalene Orsini, a Dominican nun, when she had been long suffering a great trial, and encouraged her to remain with him on the cross with that sorrow that was afflicting her. Sister Magdalene answered him complainingly: 'Oh Lord, thou didst suffer on the cross only three hours, but it is more than three years that I have been suffering this cross.' Then the Redeemer replied: 'Ah! Ignorant soul, what dost thou say? I, from the first moment I was conceived, suffered in heart what I afterwards suffered on the cross.' If, then, we too suffer any affliction and complain, let us imagine that Jesus and his mother Mary are saying to us the same words.

EXAMPLE

Father Roviglione, of the Company of Jesus, relates,[2] that a certain youth practised the devotion of visiting every day an image of the sorrowful Mary, in which she was represented with seven swords piercing her heart. One night the unhappy youth fell into mortal sin. Going next morning to visit the image, he saw in the heart of the blessed Virgin not only seven, but eight swords. As he stood gazing at this, he heard a voice saying to him, that his sin had added the eighth sword to the heart of

---

[1] Ille doloris gladius Virgini omni hora tanto se propius approximabat, quanto Filius passionis tempori magis appropinquabat. Fer. 6, lect. 2, c. 16.

[2] Fasc. di Rose, p. 2, c. 2.

Mary. This softened his hard heart; he went immediately to confession, and through the intercession of his advocate, recovered the divine grace.

PRAYER

Oh my blessed mother, not one sword only, but as many swords as I have committed sins have I added to those seven in thy heart. Ah, my Lady, thy sorrows are not due to thee who art innocent, but to me who am guilty. But since thou hast wished to suffer so much for me, ah, by thy merits obtain for me great sorrow for my sins, and patience under the trials of this life, which will always be light in comparison with my demerits, for I have often merited hell. Amen.

On The Second Dolour Of The Flight Of Jesus Into Egypt

As the stag, wounded by an arrow, carries the pain with him wherever he goes, because he carries with him the arrow that has wounded him; thus the divine mother, after the prophecy of St Simeon, as we saw in our consideration of the first grief, always carried her sorrow with her by the continual remembrance of the passion of her Son. Ailgrin, explaining this passage of the Canticles, 'The hairs of thy head as the purple of the king bound in the channel,'[1] says: These hairs of Mary were her continual thoughts of the passion of Jesus, which kept always before her eyes the blood which was one day to flow from his wounds. 'Thy mind, oh Mary, and thy thoughts tinged in the blood of the passion of our Lord, were always moved with sorrow as if they actually saw the blood

---

[1] Et comæ capitis tui sicut purpura regis vincta canalibus. Cant. 7:5.

flowing from his wounds.'[1] Thus her Son himself was that arrow in the heart of Mary, who, the more worthy of love he showed himself to her, always wounded her the more with the sorrowful thought that she should lose him by so cruel a death. Let us now pass to the consideration of the second sword of sorrow which wounded Mary, in the flight of her infant Jesus into Egypt from the persecution of Herod.

Herod having heard that the expected Messiah was born, foolishly feared that the new-born King would deprive him of his kingdom. Hence St Fulgentius, reproving him for his folly, thus says: 'Why, oh Herod, art thou thus disturbed? This King who is born has not come to conquer kings by arms, but to subjugate them, in a wonderful manner, by his death.'[2] The impious Herod, therefore, waited to learn from the holy magi where the King was born, that he might take from him his life; but finding himself deceived by the magi, he ordered all the infants that could be found in the neighbourhood of Bethlehem to be put to death. But an angel appeared in a dream to St Joseph, and said to him: 'Arise, and take the child and his mother, and fly into Egypt.'[3] According to Gerson, immediately, on that very night, Joseph made this command known to Mary; and taking the infant Jesus, they commenced their journey, as it seems clearly from the Gospel itself: 'Who arose and took the child and his mother by night, and retired into Egypt.'[4] Oh God, as blessed Albertus Magnus says in the name of Mary, must

---

[1] Mens tua, O Maria, et cogitationes tuæ tinctæ in sanguine dominicæ passionis, sic affectæ semper fuere, quasi recenter viderent sanguinem de vulneribus profluentem. In Cant. 7:5.

[2] Quid est quod sic turbaris Herodes? Rex iste qui natus est non venit reges pugnando superare sed moriendo mirabiliter subjugare. Serm. 5, de Epiph.

[3] Surge et accipe puerum, et matrem ejus et fuge in Egyptum. Matt. 2:13.

[4] Qui consurgens accepit puerum et matrem ejus nocte, et secessit in Egyptum. Matt. 2:14.

he, then, who came to save men flee from men? '*Debet fugere qui salvator est mundi?*' And then the afflicted Mary knew that already the prophecy of Simeon, regarding her Son, was beginning to be verified: 'He is set for a sign which shall be contradicted.'[1] Seeing that scarcely is he born, when he is persecuted to death. What suffering it must have been to the heart of Mary, writes St John Chrysostom, to hear the tidings of that cruel exile of herself with her Son! 'Flee from thy friends to strangers, from the holy temple of the only true God, to the temples of demons. What greater tribulation than that a new-born child, clinging to its mother's bosom, should be forced to fly with the mother herself!'[2]

Everyone can imagine how much Mary must have suffered on this journey. It was a long distance to Egypt. Authors generally agree with Barrada[3] that it was four hundred miles; so that at least it was a journey of thirty days. The way, as St Bonaventure describes it, was 'rough, unknown, through woods, and little frequented'.[4] The season was winter, and therefore they had to travel in snow, rain, wind, and storms, and through bad and difficult roads. Mary was then fifteen years of age, a delicate virgin, unaccustomed to such journeys. They had no servant to attend them. 'Joseph and Mary,' said St Peter Chrysologus, 'had no man-servant nor maid-servant; they were themselves both masters and servants.'[5] Oh God, how piteous a spectacle it was to see that tender Virgin, with that newly born infant in her arms, wandering through this world! St Bonaventure asks,

[1] Positus est hic in signum cui contradicetur.
[2] Fuge a tuis ad extraneos, a templo ad dæmonum fana. Quæ major tribulatio, quam quod recens natus a collo matris pendens cum ipsa matre paupercula fugere cogatur?
[3] 3, Lib. 10, c. 8.
[4] Viam silvestrem, obscuram, asperam, et inhabitam.
[5] Joseph et Maria non habent famulum, non ancillam; ipsi domini et famuli.

'Where did they obtain food? Where did they rest at night? How were they lodged?'[1] What other food could they have, than a piece of hard bread which Joseph brought with him or begged in charity? Where could they have slept (particularly in the two hundred miles of desert through which they travelled, where, as authors relate, there were neither houses nor inns) except on the sand, or under some tree in the wood, in the open air, exposed to robbers, or those wild beasts with which Egypt abounded? Ah, if anyone had met these three greatest personages of the world, what would he have believed them to be but three poor, roving beggars?

They lived in Egypt, according to Brocard and Jansenius, in a district called Maturea, though, according to St Anselm, they dwelt in Heliopolis, first called Memphis, and now Cairo. And here let us consider the great poverty they must have suffered for the seven years they were there, as St Antoninus, St Thomas, and others assert. They were foreigners, unknown, without revenues, without money, without kindred; hardly were they able to support themselves by their humble labours. As they were destitute, says St Basil, it is manifest what efforts they must have made to obtain there the necessaries of life.[2] Moreover, Landolph of Saxony has written, and let it be repeated for the consolation of the poor, that so great was the poverty of Mary there, that sometimes she had not so much as a morsel of bread, when her Son, forced by hunger, asked it of her.[3]

St Matthew also relates that when Herod was dead, the angel again appeared, in a dream, to St Joseph, and directed him to return to Judea. St Bonaventure, speaking of this return,

[1] Quomodo faciebant de victu? Ubi nocte quiescebant? Quomodo hospitabantur? De Vit. Chr.
[2] Cum enim essent egeni, manifestum est quod sudores frequentabant necessaria vitæ inde sibi quærentes.
[3] Aliquando filius famem patiens panem petiit, nec unde dare mater habuit. In Vit. Christi. c. 13.

considers the greater pain of the blessed Virgin, on account of the sufferings which Jesus must have endured in that journey, having arrived at about the age of seven years—an age, says the saint, when 'he was so large that he could not be carried, and so small that he could not go without assistance.'[1]

The sight, then, of Jesus and Mary wandering like fugitives through this world, teaches us that we should also live as pilgrims on the earth, detached from the goods which the world offers us, as having soon to leave them and go to eternity. 'We have not here a lasting city, but seek one that is to come.'[2] To which St Augustine adds: Thou art a stranger, thou givest a look, and then passest on: '*Hospes es, vides et transis.*' It also teaches us to embrace crosses, for we cannot live in this world without a cross. The blessed Veronica da Binasco, an Augustinian nun, was carried in spirit to accompany Mary and the infant Jesus in this journey to Egypt, and at the end of it the divine mother said to her: 'Child, hast thou seen through what difficulties we have reached this place? Now learn that no one receives graces without suffering.' He who wishes to feel least the sufferings of this life, must take Jesus and Mary with him: '*Accipe puerum et matrem ejus.*' For him who lovingly bears in his heart this Son and this mother, all sufferings become light, and even sweet and dear. Let us then love them, let us console Mary by receiving her Son within our hearts, whom, even now, men continue to persecute with their sins.

EXAMPLE

One day the most holy Mary appeared to the blessed Colletta, a Franciscan nun, and showed her the infant Jesus

---

[1] Sic magnus est, ut portari non valeat: et sic parvus quod per se ire non potest.

[2] Non habemus hic manentem civitatem, sed futuram inquirimus. Heb. 13:14.

in a basin, torn in pieces, and then said to her: 'Thus sinners continually treat my Son, renewing his death and my sorrows; oh, my daughter, pray for them that they may be converted.'[1] Similar to this is that other vision which appeared to the venerable Sister Jane of Jesus and Mary, also a Franciscan nun. As she was one day meditating on the infant Jesus, persecuted by Herod, she heard a great noise, as of armed people, who were pursuing some one; and then appeared before her a most beautiful child, who was fleeing in great distress, and cried to her: 'My Jane, help me, hide me; I am Jesus of Nazareth, I am flying from sinners who wish to kill me, and who persecute me as Herod did: do thou save me.'[2]

PRAYER

Then, oh Mary, even after thy Son hath died by the hands of men who persecuted him unto death, have not these ungrateful men yet ceased from persecuting him with their sins, and continuing to afflict thee, oh mother of sorrows? And I also, oh God, have been one of these. Ah, my most sweet mother, obtain for me tears to weep for such ingratitude. And then, by the sufferings thou didst experience in thy journey to Egypt, assist me in the journey that I am making to eternity, that at length I may go to unite with thee in loving my persecuted Saviour, in the country of the blessed. Amen.

---

[1] Ap. P. Genev. Serv. Dol. di Mar.
[2] Loc. cit.

On The Third Dolour Of The Loss Of Jesus In The Temple

St James the Apostle has said, that our perfection consists in the virtue of patience. 'And patience hath a perfect work, that you may be perfect and entire, failing in nothing.'[1] The Lord having then given us the Virgin Mary as an example of perfection, it was necessary that she should be laden with sorrows, that in her we might admire and imitate her heroic patience. The dolour that we are this day to consider is one of the greatest which our divine mother suffered during her life, namely, the loss of her Son in the temple. He who is born blind is little sensible of the pain of being deprived of the light of day; but to him who has once had sight and enjoyed the light,

---

[1] Patientia autem opus perfectum habet, ut sitis perfecti et integri, in nullo deficientes. Jm. 1:4.

it is a great sorrow to find himself deprived of it by blindness. And thus it is with those unhappy souls who, being blinded by the mire of this earth, have but little knowledge of God, and therefore scarcely feel pain at not finding him. On the contrary, the man who, illuminated with celestial light, has been made worthy to find by love the sweet presence of the highest good, oh God, how he mourns when he finds himself deprived of it! From this we can judge how painful must have been to Mary, who was accustomed to enjoy constantly the sweet presence of Jesus, that third sword which wounded her, when she lost him in Jerusalem, and was separated from him for three days.

In the second chapter of St Luke we read that the blessed Virgin, being accustomed to visit the temple every year at the paschal season, with Joseph her spouse and Jesus, once went when he was about twelve years old, and Jesus remained in Jerusalem, though she was not aware of it, for she thought he was in company with others. When she reached Nazareth she inquired for her Son, and not finding him there, she returned immediately to Jerusalem to seek him, but did not succeed until after three days. Now let us imagine what distress that afflicted mother must have experienced in those three days in which she was searching everywhere for her Son, with the spouse in the Canticles: 'Have you seen him whom my soul loveth?'[1] But she could hear no tidings of him. Oh, with how much greater tenderness must Mary, overcome with fatigue, and yet not having found her beloved Son, have repeated those words of Ruben, concerning his brother Joseph: The boy doth not appear, and whither shall I go? *'Puer non comparet, et ego quo ibo?'* My Jesus doth not appear, and I know not what to do that I may find him; but where shall I go without my treasure? Weeping continually, she repeated during these three days with David: 'My tears have been my bread day and night, whilst it is said to me daily, Where is thy

---

[1] Num quem diligit anima mea vidistis? Cant. 3:3.

God?'[1] Wherefore Pelbart with reason says that 'during those nights the afflicted mother had no rest, but wept and prayed without ceasing to God, that he would enable her to find her Son.'[2] And, according to St Bernard, often during that time did she repeat to her Son himself the words of the spouse: 'Show me where thou feedest, where thou liest in the mid-day, lest I begin to wander.'[3] My Son, tell me where thou art, that I may no longer wander, seeking thee in vain.

Some writers assert, and not without reason, that this dolour was not only one of the greatest, but that it was the greatest and most painful of all. For in the first place, Mary in her other dolours had Jesus with her; she suffered when St Simeon uttered the prophecy in the temple; she suffered in the flight to Egypt, but always with Jesus; but in this dolour she suffered at a distance from Jesus, without knowing where he was: 'And the light of my eyes itself is not with me.'[4] Thus, with tears, she then exclaimed: Ah, the light of my eyes, my dear Jesus, is no more with me; he is far from me, I know not where he is! Origen says that through the love which this holy mother bore her Son, she suffered more at this loss of Jesus than any martyr ever suffered at death.[5] Ah, how long were these three days for Mary! They appeared three ages. Very bitter days, for there was none to comfort her. And who, she exclaimed with Jeremias, who can console me if he who could console me is far from me? And therefore my eyes are not satisfied with weeping: 'Therefore do I weep, and my eyes run

[1] Fuerunt mihi lacrymæ meæ panes die ac nocte, dum dicitur mihi quotidie, ubi est Deus tuus? Ps. 41:4.
[2] Illas noctes insomnes duxit in lacrymis, Deum deprecando, ut daret illi reperire filium.
[3] Indica, mihi ubi cubes, ubi pascas in meridie, ne vagari incipiam. Cant. 1:6.
[4] Lumen oculorum meorum, et ipse non est mecum. Ps. 27:11.
[5] Vehementer doluit, quia vehementer amabat. Plus doluit de ejus amissione, quam aliquis martyr dolorem sentiat de animæ a corpore separatione. Hom. infr. Oct. Ep.

down with water, because the comforter is far from me.'[1] And with Tobias she repeated: 'What manner of joy shall be to me who sit in darkness, and see not the light of heaven?'[2]

Secondly.—Mary well understood the cause and end of the other dolours, namely, the redemption of the world, the divine will; but in this she did not know the cause of the absence of her Son. The sorrowful mother was grieved to find Jesus withdrawn from her, for her humility, says Lanspergius, 'made her consider herself unworthy to remain with him any longer, and attend upon him on earth, and have the care of such a treasure.'[3] And perhaps she may have thought within herself, I have not served him as I ought. Perhaps I have been guilty of some neglect, and therefore he has left me. 'They sought him, lest he perchance had left them,' as Origen has said.[4] Certainly there is no greater grief for a soul that loves God than the fear of having displeased him. And therefore Mary never complained in any other sorrow but this, lovingly expostulating with Jesus after she found him: 'Son, why hast thou done so to us? Thy father and I have sought thee sorrowing.'[5] By these words she did not wish to reprove Jesus, as the heretics blasphemously assert, but only to make known to him the grief she had experienced during his absence from her, on account of the love she bore him. It was not a rebuke, says blessed Denis the Carthusian, but a loving complaint: '*Non erat increpatio, sed amorosa conquestio.*' Finally, this sword so cruelly pierced the heart of the Virgin, that the

---

[1] Idcirco ego plorans, et oculus meus deducens aquas, quia longe est a me consolator meus. Lam. 1:16.
[2] Quale gaudium erit mihi, qui in tenebris sedeo, et lumen cœli non video. Tob. 6:11.
[3] Tristabatur ex humilitate, quia arbitrabatur se indignam cui tam pretiosus commissus esset thesaurus.
[4] Quærebant eum, ne forte reliquisset eos. Ap. Corn. à Lap. in Lk. 2.
[5] Fili, quid fecisti nobis sis? Pater tuus et ego dolentes quærebamus te. Lk. 2:48.

blessed Benvenuta, desiring one day to share the pain of the holy mother in this dolour, and praying her to obtain for her this grace, Mary appeared to her with the infant Jesus in her arms; but while Benvenuta was enjoying the sight of that most beautiful child, in one moment she was deprived of it. So great was her sorrow that she had recourse to Mary, to implore her pity that it should not make her die of grief. The holy Virgin appeared to her again three days after, and said to her: 'Now learn, oh my daughter, that thy sorrow is but a small part of that which I suffered when I lost my Son.'[1]

This sorrow of Mary ought, in the first place, to serve as a comfort to those souls who are desolate and do not enjoy the sweet presence they once enjoyed of their Lord. They may weep, but let them weep in peace, as Mary wept the absence of her Son. Let them take courage, and not fear that on this account they have lost the divine favour, for God himself said to St Teresa: 'No one is lost without knowing it; and no one is deceived without wishing to be deceived.' If the Lord departs from the sight of that soul who loves him, he does not therefore depart from the heart. He often hides himself that she may seek him with greater desire and love. But those who would find Jesus must seek him, not amid the delights and pleasures of the world, but amid crosses and mortifications, as Mary sought him: We sought thee sorrowing, as she said to her Son: '*Dolentes quærebamus te.*' Learn from Mary to seek Jesus, says Origen: '*Disce a Maria quærere Jesum.*'

Moreover, in this world we should seek no other good than Jesus. Job was not unhappy when he lost all that he possessed on earth; riches, children, health, and honours, and even descended from a throne to a dunghill; but because he had God with him, even then he was happy. St Augustine, speaking of him, says: He had lost all that God had given him, but he

[1] March. Diar. 30, Ott.

had God himself: '*Perdiderat illa quæ dederat Deus, sed habebat ipsum Deum.*' Unhappy and truly wretched are those souls who have lost God. If Mary wept for the absence of her Son for three days, how ought sinners to weep who have lost divine grace, to whom God says: 'You are not my people, and I will not be yours.'[1] For sin does this, namely, it separates the soul from God: 'Your iniquities have divided between you and your God.'[2] Hence, if even sinners possess all the goods of earth and have lost God, every thing on earth becomes vanity and affliction to them, as Solomon confessed: 'Behold, all is vanity and vexation of spirit.'[3] But as St Augustine says: 'The greatest misfortune of these poor blind souls is, that if they lose an ox, they do not fail to go in search of it; if they lose a sheep, they use all diligence to find it; if they lose a beast of burden, they cannot rest; but they lose the highest good, which is God, and yet they eat and drink, and take their rest.'[4]

EXAMPLE

We read in the Annual Letters of the Society of Jesus, that in India, a young man who was just leaving his apartment in order to commit sin heard a voice, saying: 'Stop, where are you going?' He turned round and saw an image, in relief, of the sorrowful Mary, who drew out the sword which was in her breast, and said to him: 'Take this dagger and pierce my heart rather than wound my Son with this sin.' At the sound of these words the youth prostrated himself on the ground and, with deep contrition, bursting into tears, he asked and obtained from God and the Virgin pardon of his sin.

[1] Vos non populus meus, et ego non ero vester. Os. 1:19.
[2] Peccata vestra diviserunt inter vos et Deum vestrum. Isa. 69:2.
[3] Ecce universa vanitas, et afflictio spiritus. Eccl. 1:14.
[4] Perdit homo bovem, et post eum vadit: perdit ovem et sollicite eam quærit; perdit asinum, et non quiescit. Perdit homo Deum, et comedit, et bibit, et quiescit.

PRAYER

Oh blessed Virgin, why art thou afflicted, seeking thy lost Son? Is it because thou dost not know where he is? But dost thou not know that he is in thy heart? Dost thou not see that he is feeding among the lilies? Thou thyself hast said it: 'My beloved to me and I to him who feedeth among the lilies.'[1] These, thy humble, pure, and holy thoughts and affections, are all lilies, that invite the divine spouse to dwell with thee. Ah, Mary, dost thou sigh after Jesus, thou who lovest none but Jesus? Leave sighing to me and so many other sinners who do not love him, and who have lost him by offending him. My most amiable mother, if through my fault thy Son has not yet returned to my soul, wilt thou obtain for me that I may find him. I know well that he allows himself to be found by all who seek him: The Lord is good to the soul that seeketh him: '*Bonus est Dominus ... animæ quærenti illum.*'[2] Make me to seek him as I ought to seek him. Thou art the gate through which all find Jesus; through thee I too hope to find him.

---

[1] Dilectus meus mihi, et ego illi, qui pascitur inter lilia. Cant. 2:16.
[2] Lam. 3:25.

On The Fourth Dolour Of The Meeting Of Mary With Jesus, When He Went To Death

S t Bernardine says, that to form an idea of the grief of Mary in losing her Jesus by death, it is necessary to consider the love that this mother bore to this her Son. All mothers feel the sufferings of their children as their own. Hence the woman of Canaan, when she prayed the Saviour to deliver her daughter from the devil that tormented her, said to him, that he should have pity on the mother rather than on the daughter: 'Have mercy on me, oh Lord, thou son of David, my daughter is grievously troubled by a devil.'[1] But what mother ever loved a child so much as Mary loved Jesus? He was her only child,

---

[1] Miserere mei, Domine fili David, filia mea male a dæmone vexatur. Matt. 15:22.

reared amidst so many troubles and pains; a most amiable child, and most loving to his mother; a Son, who was at the same time her Son and her God; who came on earth to kindle in the hearts of all the holy fire of divine love, as he himself declared: 'I am come to cast fire on the earth, and what will I but that it be kindled?'[1] Let us consider how he must have inflamed that pure heart of his holy mother, so free from every earthly affection. In a word, the blessed Virgin herself said to St Bridget, that through love her heart and the heart of her Son was one: '*Unum erat cor meum, et cor filii mei.*' That blending of handmaid and mother, of Son and God, kindled in the heart of Mary a fire composed of a thousand flames. But afterwards, at the time of the passion, this flame of love was changed into a sea of sorrow. Hence St Bernardine says: 'All the sorrows of the world united would not be equal to the sorrow of the glorious Mary.'[2] Yes, because this mother, as St Lawrence Justinian writes: 'The more tenderly she loved, was the more deeply wounded.'[3] The greater the tenderness with which she loved him, the greater was her grief at the sight of his sufferings, especially when she met her Son, after he had already been condemned, going to death at the place of punishment, bearing the cross. And this is the fourth sword of sorrow which today we have to consider.

The blessed Virgin revealed to St Bridget, that at the time when the passion of our Lord was drawing nigh, her eyes were always filled with tears, as she thought of her beloved Son whom she was about to lose on this earth. Therefore, as she also said, a cold sweat covered her body from the fear that seized her at that prospect of approaching suffering.[4] Behold, the appointed

---

[1] Ignem veni mittere in terram, et quid volo, nisi ut accendatur. Lk. 12:49.
[2] Omnes dolores mundi, si essent simul conjuncti, non essent tanti quantus dolor gloriosæ Mariæ. Tom. iii. 5, 45.
[3] Quanto dilexit tenerius, tanto est vulnerata profundius.
[4] Imminente passione filii mei, lacrymæ erant in oculis meis, et sudor in corpore præ timore. L. 1, Rev. c. 10.

day at length arrived, and Jesus came in tears to take leave of his mother before he went to death. St Bonaventure, contemplating Mary on that night, says: Thou didst spend it without sleep, and while others slept, thou didst remain watching.[1] Morning having arrived, the disciples of Jesus Christ came to this afflicted mother, one, to bring her this tiding, another, that; but all tidings of sorrow, for in her were then verified the words of Jeremias: 'Weeping, she hath wept in the night, and her tears are on her cheeks; there is none to comfort her of all them that were dear to her.'[2] One came to relate to her the cruel treatment of her Son in the house of Caiphas; another, the insults received by him from Herod. Finally, for I omit all the rest to come to my point, St John came, and announced to Mary that the most unjust Pilate had already condemned him to death upon the cross. I say the most unjust, for, as St Leo remarks, this unjust judge condemned him to death with the same lips with which he had pronounced him innocent.[3] Ah, sorrowful mother, said St John to her, thy Son has already been condemned to death, he is already on his way, bearing himself his cross on his way to Calvary, as he afterwards related in his Gospel: 'And bearing his own cross, he went forth to that place which is called Calvary.'[4] Come, if thou dost desire to see him, and bid him a last farewell in some of the streets through which he is to pass.

Mary goes with St John, and she perceives by the blood with which the way was sprinkled, that her Son had already passed there. This she revealed to St Bridget: 'By the footsteps of my Son I traced his course, for along the way by which he

[1] Sine somno duxisti, et soporatis cæteris, vigil permansisti.
[2] Plorans ploravit in nocte, et lacrymæ in maxillis ejus; non est qui consoletur eam, ex omnibus charis ejus. Lam. 1:12.
[3] Iisdem labiis mittit ad mortem quibus eum pronuntiaverunt innocentem.
[4] Et bajulans sibi crucem exivit in eum qui dicitur Calvariæ locum. Jn. 19:17.

had passed, the ground was sprinkled with blood.'[1] St Bonaventure imagines the afflicted mother taking a shorter way, and placing herself at the corner of the street to meet her afflicted Son as he passed by.[2] This most afflicted mother met her most afflicted Son: '*Mœstissima mater mœstissimo filio occurrit,*' said St Bernard. While Mary stopped in that place how much she must have heard said against her Son by the Jews, who knew her, and perhaps also words in mockery of herself! Alas! What a commencement of sorrows was then before her eyes, when she saw the nails, the hammers, the cords, the fatal instruments of the death of her Son borne before him! And what a sword pierced her heart when, she heard the trumpet proclaiming along the way the sentence pronounced against her Son! But behold, now, after the instruments, the trumpet, and the ministers of justice had passed, she raises her eyes and sees; she sees, oh God, a young man covered with blood and wounds from head to foot, with a crown of thorns on his head, and two heavy beams on his shoulders; she looks at him and hardly knows him, saying, then, with Isaias: 'And we have seen him, and there was no sightliness.'[3] Yes, for the wounds, the bruises, and clotted blood, made him look like a leper: 'We have thought him, as it were, a leper;'[4] so that he could no longer be recognised. 'And his look was, as it were, hidden and despised, whereupon we esteemed him not.'[5] But at length love recognises him, and as soon as she knows him, ah, what was then, as St Peter of Alcantara says in his meditations, the love and fear of the heart of Mary! On the one hand, she desired to see him; on the other,

---

[1] Ex vestigiis filii mei cognoscebam incessum ejus; quo enim procedebat, apparebat terra infusa sanguine. L. 4, c. 77.
[2] Med. 6.
[3] Et vidimus eum, et non erat aspectus. Is. 53:2.
[4] Putavimus eum quasi leprosum. Is. 53:4.
[5] Et quasi absconditus vultus ejus, et despectus, unde nec reputavimus eum. Is. 53:3.

she could not endure to look upon so pitiable a sight. But at length they look at each other. The Son wipes from his eyes the clotted blood, which prevented him from seeing (as was revealed to St Bridget), and looks upon the mother; the mother looks upon the Son. Ah, looks of sorrow, which pierced, as with so many arrows, those two holy and loving souls. When Margaret, the daughter of Sir Thomas More, met her father on his way to the scaffold, she could utter only two words, oh, Father! oh, Father! and fell fainting at his feet. At the sight of her Son going to Calvary, Mary fainted not; no, because it was not fitting that this mother should lose the use of her reason, as Father Suarez remarks, neither did she die, for God reserved her for a greater grief; but if she did not die, she suffered sorrow enough to cause her a thousand deaths.

The mother wished to embrace him, as St Anselm says, but the officers of justice thrust her aside, loading her with insults, and urge onward our afflicted Lord. Mary follows. Ah, holy Virgin, where art thou going? To Calvary! And canst thou trust thyself to see him who is thy life hanging from a cross? And thy life shall be as it were hanging before thee: '*Et erit vita tua quasi pendens ante te.*'[1] Ah! My mother, stop, says St Lawrence Justinian, as if the Son himself had then spoken to her; where dost thou hasten? Where art thou going? If thou comest where I go, thou wilt be tortured with my sufferings, and I with thine.[2] But although the sight of her dying Jesus must cost her such cruel anguish, the loving Mary will not leave him. The Son goes before, and the mother follows, that she may be crucified with her Son, as William the Abbot says: 'The mother took up her cross, and followed him, that she might be crucified with him.'[3]

---

[1] Deut. 28:66.
[2] Heu quo properas, quo venis mater! Cruciatu meo cruciaberis, et ego tuo.
[3] Tollebat et mater crucem suam, et sequebatur eum, crucifigenda cum

We even pity the wild beasts: '*Ferarum etiam miseremur;*' St John Chrysostom has said. If we should see a lioness following her whelp as he was led to death, even this wild beast would call forth our compassion. And shall we not feel compassion to see Mary following her immaculate Lamb, as they are leading him to death? Let us then pity her, and endeavour also ourselves to accompany her Son and herself, bearing with patience the cross which the Lord imposes on us. Why did Jesus Christ, asks St John Chrysostom, desire to be alone in his other sufferings, but in bearing the cross wished to be helped by the Cyrenean? And he answers: 'That thou mayest understand that the cross of Christ is not sufficient without thine.'[1] The cross alone of Jesus is not enough to save us, if we do not bear with resignation also our own, even unto death.

EXAMPLE

The Saviour appeared one day to Sister Diomira, a nun, in Florence, and said to her: 'Think of me, and love me, and I will think of thee, and love thee' and at the same time he presented her with a bunch of flowers and a cross, signifying to her by this, that the consolations of the saints on this earth are always to be accompanied by the cross. The cross unites souls to God. Blessed Jerome Emilian, when he was a soldier, and leading a very sinful life, was shut up by his enemies in a tower. There, feeling deeply his misfortune, and enlightened by God to amend his life, he had recourse to the most holy Mary, and then with the help of this divine mother, he began to live the life of a saint. By this he merited to see once in heaven the high place which God had prepared for him. He became founder of the order of Sommaschi, died a saint, and has been lately beatified by the holy Church.

ipso. In Cant. 7.

[1] Ut intelligas Christi crucem non sufficere sine tua.

PRAYER

My sorrowful mother, by the merit of that grief which thou didst feel at seeing thy beloved Jesus led to death, obtain for me the grace also to bear with patience those crosses which God sends me. Happy me, if I also shall know how to accompany thee with my cross until death. Thou and Jesus, both innocent, have borne a heavy cross; and shall I a sinner, who have merited hell, refuse mine? Ah, immaculate Virgin, I hope that thou wilt help me to bear my crosses with patience. Amen.

On The Fifth Dolour Of The Death Of Jesus

And now we have to admire a new sort of martyrdom, a mother condemned to see an innocent son, whom she loved with all the affection of her heart, put to death before her eyes, by the most barbarous tortures. There stood by the cross of Jesus his mother: '*Stabat autem juxta crucem mater ejus.*' There is nothing more to be said, says St John, of the martyrdom of Mary: behold her at the foot of the cross, looking on her dying Son, and then see if there is grief like her grief. Let us stop then also today on Calvary, to consider this fifth sword that pierced the heart of Mary, namely, the death of Jesus.

As soon as our afflicted Redeemer had ascended the hill of Calvary, the executioners stripped him of his garments, and piercing his sacred hands and feet with nails, not sharp, but blunt: '*Non acutis, sed obtusis;*' as St Bernard says,[1] and to torture him more, they fastened him to the cross. When they had cruci-

[1] Serm. 2, de Pass.

fied him, they planted the cross, and thus left him to die. The executioners abandon him, but Mary does not abandon him. She then draws nearer to the cross, in order to assist at his death. 'I did not leave him,' thus the blessed Virgin revealed to St Bridget, 'and stood nearer to his cross.'[1] But what did it avail, oh Lady, says St Bonaventure, to go to Calvary to witness there the death of this Son? Shame should have prevented thee, for his disgrace was also thine, because thou wast his mother; or, at least, the horror of such a crime as that of seeing a God crucified by his own creatures, should have prevented thee.[2] But the saint himself answers: Thy heart did not consider the horror, but the suffering: '*Non considerabat cor tuum horrorem, sed dolorem.*' Ah, thy heart did not then care for its own sorrow, but for the suffering and death of thy dear Son; and therefore thou thyself didst wish to be near him, at least to compassionate him. Ah, true mother! says William the Abbot, loving mother! For not even the terror of death could separate thee from thy beloved Son.[3] But, oh God, what a spectacle of sorrow, to see this Son then in agony upon the cross, and under the cross this mother in agony, who was suffering all the pain that her Son was suffering! Behold the words in which Mary revealed to St Bridget the pitiable state of her dying Son, as she saw him on the cross: 'My dear Jesus was on the cross in grief and in agony; his eyes were sunken, half closed, and lifeless; the lips hanging, and the mouth open; the cheeks hollow, and attached to the teeth; the face lengthened, the nose sharp, the countenance sad; the head had fallen upon his breast, the hair black with blood, the stomach collapsed, the arms and legs stiff, and the whole body covered with wounds and blood.'[4]

---

[1] Ego non separabar ab eo, et stabam vicinior cruci ejus. L. 1, c. 6.
[2] Cur ivisti, O Domina, ad Calvariæ locum? cur te non retinuit pudor, horror facinoris?
[3] Plane mater, quæ nec in terrore mortis filium deserebat. Serm. 3, de Ass.
[4] L. 1, Rev. c. 10, et l. 4, c. 70.

Mary also suffered all these pains of Jesus. Every torture inflicted on the body of Jesus, says St Jerome, was a wound in the heart of the mother.[1] Any one of us who should then have been on Mount Calvary, would have seen two altars, says St John Chrysostom, on which two great sacrifices were consummating, one in the body of Jesus, the other in the heart of Mary. But rather would I see there, with St Bonaventure, one altar only, namely, the cross alone of the Son, on which, with the victim, this divine Lamb, the mother also was sacrificed. Therefore the saint interrogates her in these words: Oh Lady, where art thou? Near the cross? Nay, on the cross, thou art crucified with thy Son.[2] St Augustine also says the same thing: The cross and nails of the Son were also the cross and nails of the mother; Christ being crucified, the mother was also crucified.[3] Yes, because, as St Bernard says, love inflicted on the heart of Mary the same suffering that the nails caused in the body of Jesus.[4] Therefore, at the same time that the Son was sacrificing his body, the mother, as St Bernardine says, was sacrificing her soul.[5]

Mothers fly from the presence of their dying children; but if a mother is ever obliged to witness the death of a child, she procures for him all possible relief; she arranges the bed, that his posture may be more easy; she administers refreshments to him; and thus the poor mother relieves her own sorrows. Ah, mother, the most afflicted of all mothers! Oh Mary, it was decreed that thou shouldst be present at the death of Jesus, but it was not

---

[1] Quot læsiones in corpore Christi, tot vulnera in corde matris. Ap. Bald. to. 1, p. 499.
[2] O Domina, ubi stas? Numquid juxta crucem? Imo in cruce cum filio cruciaris? Ap. Bald. tom. 1, p. 452.
[3] Crux et clavi filii fuerunt et matris; Christo crucifixo crucifigebatur et mater.
[4] Quod in carne Christi agebant clavi, in Virginis mente affectus erga filium.
[5] Dum illi corpus, ista spiritum immolabat. To. 1, Serm. 31.

given to thee to afford him any relief. Mary heard her Son say: I thirst: '*Sitio;*' but it was not permitted her to give him a little water to quench his great thirst. She could only say to him, as St Vincent Ferrer remarks: My Son, I have only the water of my tears: '*Fili, non habeo nisi aquam lacrymarum.*'[1] She saw that her Son, suspended by three nails to that bed of sorrow, could find no rest. She wished to clasp him to her heart, that she might give him relief, or at least that he might expire in her arms, but she could not.[2] She saw that poor Son in a sea of sorrow, seeking one who could console him, as he had predicted by the mouth of the prophet: 'I have trodden the wine-press alone; I looked about and there was none to help; I sought and there was none to give aid.'[3] But who was there among men to console him, if all were his enemies? Even on the cross they cursed and mocked him on every side: 'And they that passed by blasphemed him, wagging their heads.'[4] Some said to him: 'If thou be the Son of God, come down from the cross.'[5] Some exclaimed: 'He saved others, himself he cannot save.'[6] Others said: 'If he be the King of Israel, let him now come down from the cross.'[7] The blessed Virgin herself said to St Bridget: 'I heard some call my Son a thief; I heard others call him an impostor; others said that no one deserved death more than he; and every word was to me a new sword of sorrow.'[8]

But what increased most the sorrows which Mary suffered through compassion for her Son, was to hear him complain on

---

[1] Ap. Bald. p. 456.
[2] Volebat eum amplecti sed manus frustra protensæ in se complexæ redibant. Ap. Bald. 463.
[3] Torcular calcavi solus.... Circumspexi, et non est auxiliator; quæsivi, et non fuit qui adjuvaret. Is. 63:3, 5.
[4] Prætereuntes autem blasphemabant eum moventes capita sua. Matt. 27:39.
[5] Si filius Dei es, descende de cruce.
[6] Alios salvos fecit, seipsum non potest salvum facere.
[7] Si rex Israel est, descendat nunc de cruce. Loc. cit.
[8] Rev. l. 4, c. 70.

the cross that even the eternal Father had abandoned him: 'My God, my God, why hast thou forsaken me?'[1] Words which, as the divine mother herself said to St Bridget, could never depart from her mind during her whole life.[2] Thus the afflicted mother saw her Jesus suffering on every side; she desired to comfort him, but could not. And what caused her the greatest sorrow was to see that, by her presence and her grief, she increased the sufferings of her Son. The sorrow itself, says St Bernard, that filled the heart of Mary, increased the bitterness of sorrow in the heart of Jesus.[3] St Bernard also says, that Jesus on the cross suffered more from compassion for his mother than from his own pains: he thus speaks in the name of the Virgin: I stood and looked upon him, and he looked upon me; and he suffered more for me than for himself.[4] The same saint also, speaking of Mary beside her dying Son, says, that she lived dying without being able to die: Near the cross stood his mother, speechless; living she died, dying she lived; neither could she die, because she was dead, being yet alive.[5] Passino writes that Jesus Christ himself, speaking one day to the blessed Baptista Varana, of Camerino, said to her, that he was so afflicted on the cross at the sight of his mother in such anguish at his feet, that compassion for his mother caused him to die without consolation. So that the blessed Baptista, being enlightened to know this suffering of Jesus, exclaimed: Oh my Lord, tell me no more of this thy sorrow, for I cannot bear it.

Men were astonished, says Simon of Cassia, when they saw this mother then keep silence, without uttering a complaint

[1] Deus, Deus meus, ut quid dereliquisti me? Matt. 27:46.
[2] Rev. l. 4, c. 70.
[3] Repleta matre, ad filium redundaret inundatio amaritudinis. Hom. in Ev. Stabat.
[4] Stabam ego videns eum, ipse videns me, et plus dolebat de me quam de se. Ap. Simisc. Cons. 28.
[5] Juxta crucem stabat mater, vox illi non erat; moriebatur vivens, vivebat moriens; nec mori poterat, quia vivens mortua erat. De Lament. Virg.

in this great suffering.¹ But if the lips of Mary were silent, her heart was not so; for she did not cease offering to divine justice the life of her Son for our salvation. Therefore we know that by the merits of her dolours she co-operated with Christ in bringing us forth to the life of grace, and therefore we are children of her sorrows: Christ, says Lanspergius, wished her whom he had appointed for our mother to co-operate with him in our redemption; for she herself at the foot of the cross was to bring us forth as her children.² And if ever any consolation entered into that sea of bitterness, namely, the heart of Mary, it was this one only; namely, the knowledge that by means of her sorrows, she was bringing us to eternal salvation; as Jesus himself revealed to St Bridget: 'My mother Mary, on account of her compassion and charity, was made mother of all in heaven and on earth.'³ And, indeed, these were the last words with which Jesus took leave of her before his death; this was his last remembrance, leaving us to her for her children in the person of John, when he said to her: Woman, behold thy Son: *'Mulier ecce filius tuus.'*⁴ And from that time Mary began to perform for us this office of a good mother; for, as St Peter Damian declares, the penitent thief, through the prayers of Mary, was then converted and saved: Therefore the good thief repented, because the blessed Virgin, standing between the cross of her Son and that of the thief, prayed her Son for him; thus rewarding, by this favour, his former service.⁵ For as other authors also

1   Stupebant omnes qui noverant hujus hominis matrem, quod etiam in tantæ angustiæ pressura silentium servabat.
2   Voluit eam Christus cooperatricem nostræ redemptionis adstare, quam nobis constituerat dare matrem; debebat enim ipsa sub cruce nos parere filios. Hom. 44, de Pass. Dom.
3   Maria mater mea, propter compassionem et charitatem facta est mater omnium in cœlis et in terra. L. 1, c. 31.
4   Jn. 19:26.
5   Idcirco resipuit bonus latro, quia B. Virgo inter cruces filii et latronis posita, filium pro latrone deprecabatur; hoc suo beneficio, antiquum latron-

relate, this thief, in the journey to Egypt with the infant Jesus, showed them kindness; and this same office the blessed Virgin has ever continued, and still continues to perform.

EXAMPLE

A young man in Perugia once promised the devil that if he would help him to commit a sinful act which he desired to do, he would give him his soul; and he gave him a writing to that effect, signed with his blood. The evil deed was committed, and the devil demanded the performance of the promise. He led the young man to a well, and threatened to take him body and soul to hell if he would not cast himself into it. The wretched youth, thinking that it would be impossible for him to escape from his enemy, climbed the well-side in order to cast himself into it, but terrified at the thought of death, he said to the devil that he had not the courage to throw himself in, and that, if he wished to see him dead, he himself should thrust him in. The young man wore about his neck the scapular of the sorrowing Mary; and the devil said to him: 'Take off that scapular, and I will thrust you in.' But the youth, seeing the protection which the divine mother still gave him through that scapular, refused to take it off, and after a great deal of altercation, the devil departed in confusion. The sinner repented, and grateful to his sorrowful mother, went to thank her, and presented a picture of this case, as an offering, at her altar in the new church of Santa Maria, in Perugia.[1]

PRAYER

Ah, mother, the most afflicted of all mothers, thy Son, then, is dead; thy Son so amiable, and who loved thee so much! Weep, for thou hast reason to weep. Who can ever console thee? Nothing can console thee but the thought that Jesus, by his death,

is obsequium recompensans. Ap. Salm. to. 1, tr. 47.

[1] Monum. Conv. Pec. ap. P. Sinisch. Sans. 16.

hath conquered hell, hath opened paradise, which was closed to men, and hath gained so many souls. From that throne of the cross he was to reign over so many hearts, which, conquered by his love, would serve him with love. Do not disdain, oh my mother, to keep me near to weep with thee, for I have more reason than thou to weep for the offences that I have committed against thy Son. Ah, mother of mercy, I hope for pardon and my eternal salvation, first through the death of my Redeemer, and then through the merits of thy dolours. Amen.

On The Sixth Dolour
The Piercing Of The Side
Of Jesus, And His Descent
From The Cross

'Oh, all ye that pass by the way attend, and see if there be any sorrow like to my sorrow.'[1] Devout souls, listen to what the sorrowful Mary says to you today: My beloved children, I do not wish you to console me; no, for my heart can never again be consoled on this earth after the death of my dear Jesus. If you wish to please me, this I ask of you, turn to me and see if there has ever been in the world a grief like mine, when I saw him who was all my love torn from me so cruelly. But, oh Lady, since thou dost not wish to be consoled,

---

[1] O vos omnes qui transitis per viam, attendite et videte, si est dolor sicut dolor meus. Lam. 1:12.

and hast such a thirst for suffering, I must say to thee that thy sorrows have not ended with the death of thy Son. Today thou wilt be pierced by another sword of sorrow, when thou shalt see a cruel lance piercing the side of this thy Son, already dead, and shalt receive him in thy arms after he is taken from the cross. And now we are to consider today the sixth dolour which afflicted this sorrowful mother. Attend and weep. Hitherto the dolours of Mary tortured her one by one, but today they are all united to assail her.

To make known to a mother that her child is dead, is sufficient to kindle her whole soul with love for the lost one. Some persons, in order to lighten their grief, will remind mothers whose children have died, of the displeasure they have once caused them. But if I, oh my queen, should wish to lighten thy sorrow for the death of Jesus in this way, what displeasure has he ever caused thee, that I could recall to thy mind? Ah, no; he always loved thee, obeyed thee, and respected thee. Now thou hast lost him, and who can describe thy sorrow? Do thou who hast felt it explain it. A devout author says that when our Redeemer was dead, the heart of the great mother was first engaged in accompanying the most holy soul of the Son, and presenting it to the eternal Father. I present thee, oh my God, Mary must then have said, the immaculate soul of thy and my Son, which has been obedient to thee even unto death: receive it, then, in thy arms. Thy justice is now satisfied, thy will accomplished; behold, the great sacrifice to thy eternal glory is consummated. And then turning to the lifeless members of her Jesus: Oh wounds, she said, oh loving wounds, I adore you, I rejoice with you, since through you salvation has been given to the world. You shall remain open in the body of my Son, to be the refuge of those who will have recourse to you. Oh how many, through you, shall receive the pardon of their sins, and then through you shall be inflamed to love the Sovereign Good!

That the joy of the following Paschal Sabbath should not be disturbed, the Jews wished the body of Jesus to be taken down from the cross; but because they could not take down a criminal until he was dead, they came with iron mallets to break his legs, as they had already done to the two thieves crucified with him. And Mary, while she remains weeping at the death of her Son, sees those armed men coming towards her Jesus. At this sight she first trembled with fear, then she said: Ah, my Son is already dead, cease to maltreat him, and cease to torture me a poor mother longer. She implored them not to break his legs: '*Oravit eos, ne frangerent crura,*' as St Bonaventure writes. But while she is thus speaking, oh, God!, she sees a soldier with violence brandishing a spear, and piercing the side of Jesus: 'One of the soldiers with a spear opened his side, and immediately there came out blood and water.'[1] The cross shook at the stroke of the spear, and, as was revealed to St Bridget, the heart of Jesus was divided: '*Ita ut ambæ partes essent divisæ.*'[2] There came out blood and water, for only a few drops of blood remained, and those also the Saviour wished to shed, in order to show that he had no more blood to give us. The injury of that stroke was offered to Jesus, but the pain was inflicted on Mary: Christ, says the devout Lanspergius, shared with his mother the infliction of that wound, for he received the insult and his mother the pain.[3] The holy Fathers explain this to be the very sword predicted to the Virgin by St Simeon; a sword, not of iron, but of grief, which pierced through her blessed soul in the heart of Jesus, where it always dwelt. Thus, among others, St Bernard says: 'The spear which opened his side passed through the soul of the Virgin,

---

[1] Unus militum lancea latus ejus aperuit, et continuo exivit sanguis, et aqua. Jn. 19:34.
[2] Rev. l. 2, c. 21.
[3] Divisit Christus cum matre sua hujus vulneris pœnam, ut ipse injuriam acciperet, mater dolorem.

which could not be torn from the heart of Jesus.'[1] And the divine mother herself revealed the same to St Bridget, saying: 'When the spear was drawn out, the point appeared red with blood; then I felt as if my heart were pierced when I saw the heart of my most dear Son pierced.'[2] The angel told St Bridget, that such were the sufferings of Mary, that she was saved from death only by the miraculous power of God.[3] In her other dolours she at least had her Son to compassionate her; and now she had not even him to take pity on her.

The afflicted mother, still fearing that other injuries might be inflicted on her Son, entreats Joseph of Arimathea to obtain from Pilate the body of her Jesus, that at least after his death she may be able to guard it and protect it from injuries. Joseph went to Pilate, and made known to him the sorrow and the wish of this afflicted mother; and St Anselm thinks that compassion for the mother softened the heart of Pilate, and moved him to grant her the body of the Saviour. And now Jesus is taken from the cross. Oh most holy Virgin, after thou with so great love hadst given thy Son to the world for our salvation, behold the world returns him to thee again! But oh, my God, how dost thou return him to me? said Mary to the world. My Son was white and ruddy: '*Dilectus meus candidus et rubicundus:*' but thou hast returned him to me blackened with bruises, and red, not with a ruddy colour, but with the wounds thou hast inflicted upon him; he was beautiful, now there is no more beauty in him; he is all deformity. All were enamoured with his aspect, now he excites horror in all who look upon him. Oh, how many swords,

---

[1] Lancea quæ ipsius latus aperuit, animam Virginis pertransivit, quæ inde nequibat avelli. De Lament. Virg.

[2] Cum retraheretur hasta, apparuit cuspis rubea sanguine. Tunc mihi videbatur quod quasi cor meum perforaretur, cum vidissem cor filii mei charissimi perforatum. Rev. c. 10.

[3] Non parvum miraculum a Deo factum est, quod B. Virgo tot doloribus sauciata spiritum non exhalarit.

says St Bonaventure, pierced the soul of this mother, when she received the body of her Son after it was taken from the cross: '*O quot gladii animam matris pertransierunt!*' Let us consider what anguish it would cause any mother to receive the lifeless body of a son! It was revealed to St Bridget, that to take down the body of Jesus, three ladders were placed against the cross. Those holy disciples first drew out the nails from the hands and feet and, according to Metaphrastes, gave them in charge to Mary. Then one supported the upper part of the body of Jesus, the other the lower, and thus took it down from the cross. Bernardine de Bustis describes the afflicted mother as raising herself, and extending her arms to meet her dear Son; she embraces him, and then sits down at the foot of the cross. She sees his mouth open, his eye shut, she examines the lacerated flesh, and those exposed bones; she takes off the crown, and sees the cruel injury made by those thorns, in that sacred head; she looks upon those pierced hands and feet, and says: Ah, my Son, to what has the love thou didst bear to men reduced thee! But what evil hast thou done to them, that they have treated thee so cruelly? Thou wast my father, Bernardine de Bustis imagines her to say, my brother, my spouse, my delight, my glory, my all.[1] Oh, my Son, behold how I am afflicted, look upon me and console me; but thou dost look upon me no more. Speak, speak to me but one word, and console me; but thou dost speak no more, for thou art dead. Then turning to those barbarous instruments, she said: Oh cruel thorns, oh nails, oh merciless spear, how could you thus torture your Creator? But what thorns, what nails? Alas! Sinners, she exclaimed, it is you who have thus cruelly treated my Son.

Thus Mary spoke and complained of us. But if now she were capable of suffering, what would she say? What grief would she feel to see that men, after the death of her Son, continue to

---

[1] Tu mihi pater eras, tu frater, sponsus, meæ deliciæ, mea gloria, tu mihi omnia eras.

torment and crucify him by their sins! Let us no longer give pain to this sorrowful mother; and if we also have hitherto grieved her by our sins, let us now do what she directs. She says to us: Return, ye transgressors, to the heart: *'Redite, prævaricatores, ad cor.'*[1] Sinners, return to the wounded heart of my Jesus; return as penitents, for he will receive you. Flee from him to him, she continues to say with Guerric the Abbot; from the Judge to the Redeemer, from the tribunal to the cross.[2] The Virgin herself revealed to St Bridget that she closed the eyes of her Son when he was taken down from the cross, but she could not close his arms: *'Ejus brachia flectere non potui.'* Jesus Christ giving us to understand by this, that he desired to remain with open arms to receive all penitent sinners who return to him. Oh world, continues Mary, behold, then, thy time is the time of lovers: *'Et ecce, tempus tuum, tempus amantium.'*[3] Now that my Son, oh world, has died to save thee, this is no longer for thee a time of fear, but of love; a time to love him who has desired to suffer so much in order to show thee the love he bore thee. Therefore, says St Bernard, is the heart of Jesus wounded that, through the visible wound, the invisible wound of love may be seen.[4] If, then, concludes Mary, in the words of the Abbot of Celles, my Son has wished his side to be opened that he might give thee his heart,[5] it is right, oh man, that thou shouldst give him thy heart. And if you wish, oh children of Mary, to find a place in the heart of Jesus without fear of being cast out, go, says Ubertino of Casale, go with Mary, for she will obtain grace for you;[6] and in the following example we have a beautiful proof of this.

[1] Is. 46:8.
[2] Ab ipso fuge ad ipsum, a judice ad redemptorem, a tribunali ad crucem.
[3] Ezech. 16:8.
[4] Propterea vulneratum est cor Christi, ut per vulnus visibile vulnus amoris invisibilis videatur. Serm. de pass. Dom.
[5] Præ nimio amore aperuit sibi latus, ut præberet cor suum.
[6] Filii hujus matris, ingredite um ipsa intra penetralia cordis Jesu.

EXAMPLE

The Disciple relates[1] that there was once a poor sinner who, among other crimes, had killed his father and a brother, and therefore became a fugitive. Happening to hear one day during Lent, a sermon upon the divine mercy, he went to the preacher himself to make his confession. The confessor having heard his crimes, sent him to an altar of the sorrowful mother to pray that she might obtain for him compunction and pardon of his sins. The sinner obeyed, and began to pray, when behold, suddenly overpowered by contrition, he falls down dead. On the following day when the priest recommended to the people to pray for the deceased, a white dove appeared in the church and let fall a card at the feet of the priest. He took it up, and found these words written on it: 'The soul of the dead, when it left the body, immediately went to paradise; and do you continue to preach the infinite mercy of God.'

PRAYER

Oh afflicted Virgin! Oh soul, great in virtues and great also in sorrows! For both arise from that great fire of love thou hast for God; thou whose heart can love nothing but God; ah Mother, have pity on me, for I have not loved God, and I have so much offended him. Thy sorrows give me great confidence to hope for pardon. But this is not enough; I wish to love my Lord, and who can better obtain this for me than thou—thou who art the mother of fair love? Ah Mary, thou dost console all, comfort me also. Amen.

---

[1] Promt. Ex. V. Miser.

On The Seventh Dolour The Burial Of The Body Of Jesus

When a mother is by the side of a suffering and dying child, she no doubt then feels and suffers all his pains; but when the afflicted child is really dead and about to be buried, and the sorrowful mother takes her last leave of him, oh God!, the thought that she is to see him no more is a sorrow that exceeds all other sorrows. Behold, the last sword of sorrow which we are to consider, when Mary, after being present at the death of her Son upon the cross, after having embraced his lifeless body, was finally to leave him in the sepulchre, never more to enjoy his beloved presence.

But that we may better understand this last dolour, let us return to Calvary, again to look upon the afflicted mother, who still holds, clasped in her arms, the lifeless body of her Son. Oh my Son, she seems then to continue to say in the words of Job, my Son, thou art changed to be cruel towards me: '*Mutatus es mihi in crudelem.*'[1] Yes, for all thy beauty, grace, virtue, and loveliness, all the signs of special love thou hast shown me, the peculiar favours thou hast bestowed on me, are all changed into so many darts of sorrow, which the more they have inflamed my love for thee, so much the more cause me cruelly to feel the pain of having lost thee. Ah, my beloved Son, in losing thee I have lost all. Thus St Bernard speaks in her name: 'Oh truly begotten of God, thou wast to me a father, a son, a spouse; thou wast my life! Now I am deprived of my father, my spouse, and my Son, for with my Son whom I have lost, I lose all things.'[2]

Thus Mary, clinging to her Son, was dissolved in grief; but those holy disciples, fearing lest this poor mother would expire there through agony, went to take the body of her Son from her arms, to bear it away for burial. Therefore, with reverential force they took him from her arms, and having embalmed him, wrapped him in a linen cloth already prepared, upon which our Lord wished to leave to the world his image impressed, as may be seen at the present day in Turin. And now they bear him to the sepulchre. The sorrowful funeral train sets forth; the disciples place him on their shoulders; hosts of angels from heaven accompany him; those holy women follow him; and the afflicted mother follows in their company her Son to the grave. When they had reached the appointed place, how gladly would Mary have buried herself there alive with her Son! 'Oh how willingly,' said the Virgin to St Bridget, 'would I have remained there alive with my Son, if it had been his will!'[3] But since this was not

---

[1] C. xxx. 21.

[2] O vere Dei nate, tu nihi pater, tu mihi filius, tu mihi sponsus, tu mihi anima eras! Nunc orbor patre, viduor sponso, desolor filio, uno perdito filio omnia perdo. De Lam. V. Mar.

[3] O quam libenter tunc posita fuissem viva cum filio meo, si fuisset voluntas ejus! Rev. l. 1.

the divine will, the authors relate that she herself accompanied the sacred body of Jesus into the sepulchre, where, as Baronius narrates, they deposited the nails and the crown of thorns. In raising the stone to close the sepulchre, the disciples of the Saviour had to turn to the Virgin, and say to her: Now, oh Lady, we must close the sepulchre; have patience, look upon thy Son and take leave of him for the last time. Then, oh my beloved Son, must the afflicted mother have said, then shall I see thee no more? Receive, then, this last time that I look upon thee, receive the last farewell from me thy dear mother, and receive my heart which I leave buried with thee. The Virgin, says St Fulgentius, earnestly desired that her soul should be buried with the body of Christ.[1] And Mary herself made this revelation to St Bridget: 'I can truly say, that at the burial of my Son, one sepulchre contained as it were two hearts.'[2]

Finally, they take the stone and close up in the holy sepulchre the body of Jesus, that great treasure, greater than any in heaven and on earth. And here let us remark that Mary left her heart buried with Jesus, because Jesus was all her treasure: 'Where your treasure is, there will your heart be also.'[3] And where shall we keep our hearts buried? With creatures? In the mire? And why not with Jesus, who, although he has ascended to heaven, has wished to remain, not dead but alive, in the most holy sacrament of the altar, precisely in order that he may have with him and possess our hearts? But let us return to Mary. Before quitting the sepulchre, according to St Bonaventure, she blessed that sacred stone, saying: Oh happy stone that doth now enclose that body which was contained nine months in my womb, I bless thee, and envy thee; I leave thee to guard my Son

---

[1] Animam cum corpore Christi contumulari Virgo vehementer exoptavit.
[2] Vere dicere possum, quod sepulto filio meo quasi duo corda in uno sepulchro fuerunt. Rev. l. 2, c. 21.
[3] Ubi thesaurus vester est, ibi et cor vestrum erit. Lk. 12:34.

for me, who is my only good, my only love. And then turning to the eternal Father, she said: Oh Father, to thee I recommend him, who is thy Son and mine; and thus bidding a last farewell to her Son, and to the sepulchre, she returned to her own house. This poor mother went away so afflicted and sad, according to St Bernard, that she moved many to tears even against their will: '*Multos etiam invitos ad lacrymas provocabat;*' so that wherever she passed, all wept who met her: '*Omnes plorabant qui obviabant ei,*' and could not restrain their tears. And he adds, that those holy disciples, and the women who accompanied her, mourned for her even more than for their Lord.[1]

St Bonaventure says, that her two sisters covered her with a mourning cloak: The sisters of our Lady wrapped her in a veil as a widow, covering as it were her whole countenance.[2] And he also says that passing, on her return, before the cross, still wet with the blood of her Jesus, she was the first to adore it: Oh holy cross, she exclaimed, I kiss thee and adore thee; for thou art no longer an infamous wood, but a throne of love, and an altar of mercy, consecrated by the blood of the divine Lamb, who has been sacrificed upon thee, for the salvation of the world. She then leaves the cross and returns to her house; there the afflicted mother casts her eyes around, and no longer sees her Jesus; but instead of the presence of her dear Son, all the memorials of his holy life and cruel death are before her. There she is reminded of the embraces she gave her Son in the stable of Bethlehem, of the conversations held with him for so many years in the shop of Nazareth: she is reminded of their mutual affection, of his loving looks, of the words of eternal life that came forth from that divine mouth. And then comes before her the fatal scene of that very day; she sees those nails, those thorns, that lacerated

---

[1] Super ipsam potius, quam super Dominum plangebant.
[2] Sorores Dominæ velaverunt eam tamquam viduam; cooperientes quasi totum vultum.

flesh of her Son, those deep wounds, those uncovered bones, that open mouth, those closed eyes. Alas! what a night of sorrow was that night for Mary! The sorrowful mother turned to St John, and said mournfully: Ah, John, where is thy Master? Then she asked of Magdalen: Daughter, tell me where is thy beloved? Oh God! who has taken him from us? Mary weeps, and all those who are with her weep. And thou, oh my soul, dost thou not weep! Ah, turn to Mary, and say to her with St Bonaventure: 'Let me, oh my Lady, let me weep; thou art innocent, I am guilty.'[1] At least entreat her to permit thee to weep with her: '*Fac ut tecum lugeam.*' She weeps for love, and thou dost weep through sorrow for thy sins. And thus weeping, thou mayest have the happy lot of him of whom we read in the following example.

EXAMPLE

Father Engelgrave relates,[2] that a certain religious was so tormented by scruples, that sometimes he was almost driven to despair, but having great devotion to Mary, the mother of sorrows, he had recourse to her in the agony of his spirit, and was much comforted by contemplating her dolours. Death came, and the devil tormented him more than ever with scruples, and tempted him to despair. When, behold our merciful mother, seeing her poor son so afflicted, appeared to him, and said to him: 'And why, oh my son, art thou so overcome with sorrow, thou who hast so often consoled me by thy compassion for my sorrows?[3] Be comforted,' she said to him; 'Jesus sends me to thee to console thee; be comforted, rejoice, and come with me to paradise.' And at these words the devout religious tranquilly expired, full of consolation and confidence.

---

[1] Sine, Domina mea, sine me flere; tu innocens es, ego sum reus.
[2] Dom infra oct Nat. s. 2.
[3] Et tu, fili mi, cur mœrore conficeris, qui in mœrore meo toties me consolatus es?

PRAYER

My afflicted mother, I will not leave thee alone to weep; no, I wish to keep thee company with my tears. This grace I ask of thee today: obtain for me a continual remembrance of the passion of Jesus, and of thine also, and a tender devotion to them, that all the remaining days of my life may be spent in weeping for thy sorrows, oh my mother, and for those of my Redeemer. I hope that these dolours will give me the confidence and strength not to despair at the hour of my death, at the sight of the offences I have committed against my Lord. By these must I obtain pardon, perseverance, paradise, where I hope to rejoice with thee, and sing the infinite mercy of my God through all eternity: thus I hope, thus may it be. Amen, amen.

* * *

Whoever wishes to practise the devotion of reciting the chaplet of the dolours of Mary, will find it at the end of the book. I composed this many years since, and insert it anew here for the convenience of the servants of Mary, whom I pray in their charity to recommend me to her when they meditate upon her dolours.

'Oh Lady, who dost ravish the hearts of men with thy sweetness, hast thou not ravished mine? Oh, ravisher of hearts, when wilt thou restore to me my heart? Do with it as with thine own, and place it in the side of thy Son. Then I shall possess what I hope for, because thou art our hope.'[1]

---

[1] O Domina, quæ rapis corda hominum dulcore, nonne cor meum rapuisti? O raptrix cordium, quando mihi restitues cor meum? Guberna illud cum tuo, et in latere filii colloca. Tunc possidebo quod spero, quia tu es spes nostra. S. Bernard. Med. in Salv. Reg. ap. s. Bon. Stim. c. 19, part. 3.

Little Rosary Of The Seven Dolours Of Mary

℣. Incline unto mine aid, oh God.
℟. O Lord, make haste to help me.
Glory be etc.
Oh my mother, enable my heart to share
thy sorrow for the death of thy Son.

First Dolour.—I pity thee, oh my afflicted mother, on account of the first sword of sorrow that pierced thee, when in the temple, by the prophecy of St Simeon, all the cruel sufferings that men would inflict on thy beloved Jesus were represented to thee, which thou hadst already learned from the holy Scriptures, even to his death before thy eyes upon the infamous wood of the cross, exhausted of blood and abandoned by all, and thou without the power to defend or relieve him. By that bitter memory, then, which for so many years afflicted thy heart, I pray thee, oh my queen, to obtain for me the grace that always in life and in death I may keep impressed upon my heart the passion of Jesus and thy sorrows.

Our Father, Hail Mary, Glory be to God, etc., Oh my mother, ec., as above. *Which verse must always be repeated at the end of each dolour.*

Second Dolour.—I pity thee, oh my afflicted mother, on account of the second sword that pierced thee when thou didst behold thy innocent Son, so soon after his birth, threatened with death by those very men for whom he had come into the world; so that thou wast obliged to flee with him by night secretly into Egypt. By the many hardships, then, that thou, a delicate young virgin, in company with thy exiled infant, didst endure in the long and wearisome journey through rough and desert countries, and in thy sojourn in Egypt, where, being unknown and a stranger, thou didst live all those years poor and despised, I pray thee, oh my beloved Lady, to obtain for me the grace to suffer with patience, in thy company till death, the trials of this miserable life, that I may be able in the next to be preserved from the eternal sufferings of hell deserved by me. **Our Father, etc.**

Third Dolour.—I pity thee, oh my afflicted mother, on account of the third sword that pierced thy heart at the loss of thy dear son, Jesus, who remained absent from thee in Jerusalem for three days, when not seeing thy beloved one by thy side, and not knowing the cause of his absence, I conceive, my loving queen, how in these nights thou didst not repose, and didst naught but sigh for him who was thy only good. By the sighs, then, of those three days, for thee so long and bitter, I pray thee to obtain for me the grace never to lose my God; that I may always live closely united to God, and thus united with him depart from this world. **Our Father, etc.**

Fourth Dolour.—I pity thee, my afflicted mother, on account of the fourth sword that pierced thy heart, in seeing thy Jesus condemned to death, bound with ropes and chains, covered with blood and wounds, crowned with thorns, and falling under the weight of the heavy cross which he bore on his bleeding back when going like an innocent lamb to die for love of us. Thine eye then met his eye, and your glances were so many cruel arrows with which each wounded the loving heart of the other. By this great grief, then, I pray thee to obtain for me the grace to live wholly resigned to the will of my God, joyfully bearing my cross with Jesus to the last moment of my life. **Our Father, etc.**

Fifth Dolour.—I pity thee, oh my afflicted mother, on account of the fifth sword that pierced thy heart, when on Mount Calvary thou didst behold thy beloved son, Jesus, dying slowly before thy eyes, amid so many insults, and in anguish, on that hard bed of the cross, without being able to give him even the least of those comforts which the greatest criminals receive at the hour of death. And I pray thee by the anguish which thou, oh my most loving mother, didst suffer together with thy dying Son, and by the tenderness thou didst feel when, for the last time, he spoke to thee from the cross, and taking leave of thee, left all of us to thee in the person of St John, as thy children; and thou, still constant, didst behold him bow his head and expire; I pray thee to obtain for me the grace, by thy crucified love, to live and die crucified to every thing in this world, in order to live only to God through my whole life, and thus to enter one day paradise, to enjoy him face to face. **Our Father, etc.**

Sixth Dolour.—I pity thee, oh my afflicted mother, on account of the sixth sword which pierced thy heart, when thou didst see the kind heart of thy Son pierced through and through after his death—a death endured for those ungrateful men, who, even after his death, were not satisfied with the tortures they had inflicted upon him. By this cruel sorrow, then, which was wholly thine, I pray thee to obtain for me the grace to abide in the heart of Jesus, who was wounded and opened for me; in that heart, I say, which is the beautiful abode of love, where all the souls who love God repose; and that living there, I may never love or think of any thing but God. Most holy Virgin, thou canst do it; from thee I hope for it. **Our Father, etc.**

Seventh Dolour.—I pity thee, my afflicted mother, on account of the seventh sword that pierced thy heart, on seeing in thy arms thy Son who had just expired, no longer fair and beautiful as thou didst once receive him in the stable of Bethlehem, but covered with blood, livid, and lacerated by wounds which exposed his very bones. My Son, thou saidst, my Son, to what has love brought thee? And when he was borne to the sepulchre, thou didst wish to accompany him thyself, and help to put him in the tomb with thy own hands; and, bidding him a last farewell, thou hast left thy loving heart buried with thy Son. By all the anguish of thy pure soul, obtain for me, oh mother of fair love, pardon for the offences that I have committed against my God, whom I love, and of which I repent with my whole heart. Wilt thou defend me in temptations? Assist me at the hour of my death, that, being saved by the merits of Jesus and thine, I may come one day, with thy aid, after this miserable exile, to sing in paradise the praises of Jesus and thine through all eternity. Amen. **Our Father, etc.**

℣. Pray for us, oh most sorrowful Virgin;
℟. That we may be worthy of the promises of Christ.

Let us Pray.
Oh God, at whose passion, according to the prophecy of Simeon, the sword of sorrow pierced through the most sweet

soul of the glorious virgin and mother, Mary, grant that we, who commemorate and reverence her dolours, may experience the blessed effect of thy passion, who livest and reignest world without end. Amen.

www.ingramcontent.com/pod-product-compliance
Lightning Source LLC
Chambersburg PA
CBHW032359100526
44587CB00010BA/587